The Evolution of Charlie Darwin

Partner With Your Dog Using

Positive Training

Beth Duman, CPDT-KA

The Evolution of Charlie Darwin – Partner With Your Dog Using Positive Training

Published by Earth Voices Publishing
2512 Sue Drive
Howell, Michigan 48855
www.EarthVoices.net

Beth Duman is available for consultation, lectures and workshops. She can be contacted through her website: www.EarthVoices.net

Library of Congress Control Number: 2011928203

ISBN-13: 978-1461153894
ISBN-10: 1461153891

DEDICATION

This book is dedicated to the memory of my friend and mentor, Princess Anja the Wonder Dog

Your dog does not understand right and wrong.

Your dog understands safe and dangerous. You want to always be "safe", not "dangerous".

Your job is to prevent behavior you do not want and reward behavior you do want.

When your dog barks or growls, she is more likely unsure, scared or defensive than brave or protective.

Your dog must build her confidence with a variety of humans, situations, and other dogs.

You must protect your dog from humans, situations, or other dogs that might frighten her or cause her to become defensive.

You are your dog's guide into a culture totally foreign to her own.

CONTENTS

FOREWORD

If training the difficult dogs makes you a better trainer, then Beth Duman should win a prize for having learned more from problem dogs than most trainers ever could. For as long as I've known Beth, she's been a magnet for "challenging dogs." After raising a captive wolf, she went on to have a Husky, and several "hand-me-down" Belgian Sheepdogs, at least one of which the breeder hung onto for way too long, until it became afraid of everything outside its own crate. The next dog she adopted was the offspring of a feral dog running loose in the swampy woods behind her house. At the age of about 16 weeks, Beth was able to capture this wild little thing, and somehow she turned "Anja," the "Smooth-coated, Miniature North-American Swamp Dog" into an amazing pet. Next, she adopted a real, bona-fide African Village Dog (straight from the African Village), and managed to turn "Killer Kaddi" into a house pet and therapy dog. A glutton for punishment, she found a stray at the local shelter, who seemed very smart, but was guarding her "babies" (the stuffed animals she had stolen from around the neighborhood), and was deemed unsafe. She was also a chronic runaway. Beth tried hard to find someone else to adopt this dog and give her a chance, but, at last, she did so herself. Beth managed to turn Lacey around, as well. With all of the education her past dogs had given her, Beth decided that her next dog would be one that didn't have all of the setbacks of her others.

She wanted something relatively smart, like a Border Collie, and "undamaged" by the baggage of his or her previous life. She wanted to start with a younger dog this time, so that she could take advantage of that all-important early socialization opportunity. This next dog would be easy to train, and would think the sun shone out of Beth's eyes.

The pet-finder ad said "Baby Border Collie." "Woody" turned out to be neither a baby, nor a Border Collie, nor even partly a Border Collie. My guess was that he was mostly Beagle and Springer Spaniel. This dog remained intact for way too long, and he considered it his duty to perform the nasty habit of marking (urinating) on the entire world. I told Beth she'd be crazy to adopt this dog, but he was kind of cute, and she caved and took him home.

But, rather than considering this to be yet another adoption that should never have been, she decided to make lemonade out of the lemon. Renaming him "Charlie," she decided to chronicle his training, which would begin with a diamond-in-the-rough "Borderless Collie" (due also to the fact that no mere fence could contain him), and evolve into a wonderful family pet. And that's how the "Evolution of Charlie Darwin" started.

In this excellent book, you will not only read about the metamorphosis of a throw-away dog, but you will be introduced to the tools that took him from zero to hero. This information will help you improve the relationship you have with your own dog. Beth will arm you with the tools necessary to take your dog from being just some animal that lives at your address, to being a cherished family member with whom you can communicate and share meaningful experiences. If everyone possessed this "owner's manual for dogs," there would be far fewer dogs tossed out the way Charlie was.

Lucky Charlie—because Beth found him, and lucky you, because he was the impetus for her writing this book. I hope you appreciate it as much as I did. She has such a wealth of information to share. Read and enjoy the same journey from merely coexisting to being BFF's (Best Friends FOREVER) with your own dog.

Lonnie Olson, Founder

Dog Scouts of America

www.DogScouts.org

ACKNOWLEDGMENTS

Positive dog trainers are some of the nicest people you'll ever meet. Because we strive to make the world a kinder, gentler place through our training, we also are dedicated to interacting with people the same way.

Ask a positive trainer for help and you'll find friends who are ready to support and offer any assistance they can. My growth as a trainer has included input from many sources. I've attended many training workshops and conferences, watched way too many dog training videos, and spent countless hours mulling training issues with my trainer friends.

Throughout the book, I'll be pointing you to other resources where you can continue to build your training skills and grow in your relationship with your dog. I thank those resource people for being my guides along my journey.

I especially thank some of my closest training friends, Lonnie Olson, the founder of Dog Scouts of America, who first inspired Bob and me to rehabilitate our snappy rescue Belgian Sheepdog, Dart, through play and agility rather than forceful confrontational training methods. My many friends at Wolf Park have challenged me by using positive training methods in handling the wolves. Chris Bach has been a wonderful mentor who has shared her deep friendship along with very skilled training pointers. Brenda Aloff is the funniest trainer I know who convinced me to self-publish rather than deal with the quirks of the big publishing companies. I am grateful to my dear friend Maggie who is always there to talk through training challenges. I thank Nancy Bailey, an amazing trainer and friend who knew I had to write a book and encouraged me along the way. Thanks to my mom, Luise Runkel, Jill Moore, Pat Convery, Connie Todd, Deb Evens, Dr. Jackie Pozniak, Betty Huerta and Lonnie Olson for wading through my typos and poor grammar to edit my transcript.

I need to thank my current dogs, Reggie, Lacey, Kaddi and Charlie Darwin for putting up with a very boring Mom who can spend far too much time staring at the computer. These quirky friends continue to hone my training skills and patience. And, of course, I thank my life partner Bob for always supporting my new ventures and being there to cook supper and feed the dogs when I'm over-scheduled and on a roll!

PHOTO CREDITS & MORE THANKS

Jim Ridley – Dedication & page 190

Peggy Hodgson – Cover, pages 42, 92, 129, & 180

City of Ft. Wayne Animal Care and Control – page 3 (photo 2)

Monty Sloan – pages 1 & 20

Carole Sharrow – pages 5 & 18

Therri O'Dea – page 10

Dog Scouts of America – pages 16, 30, 53 (photo 1), 63 (photo 2), 70, 93, 116, & 162

Joanne Weber – page 23

Karla Trombley - pages 24, 27 (photo 1), 62, 97, 99, 131, 132, & 147

Bob Duman – pages 33, 79, 100, 112, 138, 171, 177, 181, & 185 (photo 1)

Mary Kotnik – page 35

Stephanie Thomas – page 48

Steve Whitney – page 86

Dave Dillman – 96

Cindy Ringwald – page 104

Jordan Hoffman – pages 122, 185 (photo 3), 186, & 191

Jacquie Read – page 145

Kate Krull – pages 169 & 170 (photo 1)

Jodi Ayers – page 172

Bob Starr – page 176

Diana Kohler – page 178

Martha Thierry for her artistic help on the cover and the photo on the back cover

All other photos by the author

Special thanks to the Trombley family for taking extra time to use their pup Buzz for a photo shoot , Dick and Marie Steele for their extra patience with Darse so we could include her in the book, Josephine Busch and Blaze for showing off their expertise at *Chin*, Teddy and Cindy Ringwald for demonstrating *Yielding to Pressure,* and Stephanie Thomas and Emery for their demonstration of the Gentle Leader.™ Thanks to all my friends and clients who so graciously shared stories about their canine friends. Special thanks to the kids of All Saints Church for sharing their love with Kaddi.

More thanks to The City of Ft. Wayne Animal Care and Control who graciously sheltered Charlie when his former owners could no longer keep him, and the North Star Border Collie Rescue who worked to find him an adoptive home.

1
GETTING STARTED – HOW TO USE THIS BOOK

Are you thinking of getting a dog, or have you recently added a new furry friend to your family and are now going bonkers wondering why you ever made such a crazy decision? Are you a trainer who's looking for some more ideas to use with your clients? This book is an outgrowth of the training handouts I've been using with my dog training clients. It's also a training journal of my first year with a funny little rescue dog named Charlie Darwin.

You'll find information in a number of formats to fit your learning style and interest:

❖ Short training essays with training ideas and background theory – these will give you the basics of working with your dog.

❖ Diary entries about dear Charlie – follow the joys and frustrations of our first year with this cute little guy.

❖ Photo descriptions of training games.

❖ References for further reading - you'll also find a full bibliography in the appendix section of the book.

❖ Testimonials from some of my training clients who've used my training materials and games successfully with their own dogs.

The characters you'll meet along the way:

Kaddi:
Kaddi is actually responsible for much of the content of this book and my understanding of how dogs' brains see the world. Kaddi is a garbage-eating scavenger pariah dog from The Gambia, West Africa. My dear daughter brought Kaddi and her brother Dowda back from the village where she lived while she

Dr. Ray Coppinger, Beth & Kaddi

was in the Peace Corps. She found them abandoned in a small barn. To understand Kaddi, you need to know a bit about the history of dogs. Sure, we all know they came from wolves, but that most likely didn't happen by our ancestors adopting wild wolf puppies. Dr. Ray Coppinger has

To learn more about the possible history of domestic dogs, check out **Dogs: A Startling New Understanding of Canine Origin, Behavior & Evolution** by Ray Coppinger

postulated that the original dogs were probably wolves that learned to scavenge garbage from around human villages. Kaddi comes from a society where dogs still live that way. They don't have names or owners who dote over them. They hang around people surviving by eating human waste (yes, I really mean human waste!) and whatever else they can find to stay alive. To put it nicely, Kaddi is *not* a nice dog. She is genetically a survivor who will do what it takes to get what she needs, even if that means looking very nasty. She's easily scared and remembers scary things forever. We've honed our training skills learning to live with her and managing all her fears and idiosyncrasies.

Lacey:

Bob always hoped that I'd dye my hair red and let it grow long. That's never going to happen, so instead, Bob's prayers have been answered now that Lacey has become his soul mate and bed warmer. Lacey spent months living in the bushes next to a nearby freeway. No one could catch her even though the caring neighbors put food out for her daily. Eventually Rita, a very caring animal control officer, drugged her and brought her into the dog pound. Rita called me in a panic when her director wanted to immediately euthanize this crazed wild dog. So, guess who ended up with Lacey, the most hyper, fruity dog on the planet? Lacey was the test pilot for many of the calming games in this book. She is now the therapy dog for the special needs kids in our community. The students are now baking and selling "Lacey Love Dog Cookies" to fund their school activities. She loves her "kids" and they all love her!

Lacey is helping sell her cookies at the school holiday bazaar

Reggie:

Reggie is a testament to why you don't want to use scary methods to train your dog. He's a gorgeous Belgian Tervuren who learned that doing nothing is the safest way to live with humans. I suspect his former owners used the "shake can" method to control his puppy exuberance. Maybe you've heard of the training method that suggests you put some pebbles in an old pop can and then lob the can near your pup to scare him

Reggie is gorgeous and very sweet!

away from whatever mischief he's getting into.

Reggie came to us knowing two tricks: running in the other direction if we extended a friendly hand toward him, and hiding under the kitchen table, doing nothing at all. Reggie has taught me to be a very patient trainer, to do my training in mini-steps — to break down each skill into the most miniscule increments.

Reggie is now a friendly gentle giant who has learned many tricks and has attained the highest honor in Dog Scouts, an Honor Scout. He is a very dear soul who knows he's very beautiful!

> To learn more about having a Dog Scout
> in your family, go to www.DogScouts.org

Princess Anja the Wonder Dog:

Dear Anja passed over a year ago but I had to make her part of this training journal because she was the canine friend who made me the trainer I am today. Anja started out her life as a feral dog roaming the river valley at the back of our property. I captured her in the swamp when she was about four months old. She went on to prove all the naysayers wrong who insisted she'd never amount to anything because of her wild unsocialized puppyhood. Anja became my working partner, friend and the best trick dog on the planet. I still miss her.

No, that's not a real frog in Anja's mouth!

Charlie B. Darwin (Yes, his middle name is Beagle!):

When my dear friend Anja died, there was a hole in my heart and a space on my car seat that needed to be filled. I also needed a dog who had the natural ability to help me do public training demonstrations.

My requirements for my ideal new dog:

1. He had to be a puppy so I could start from scratch in training him the right way

2. He had to fit on my car seat. Yes, that really was a requirement — traveling with four dogs in a van has to be physically possible.

3. He had to like people and other dogs

**Charlie's shelter photo on Petfinder.com
I should have looked more closely and
noticed he was sitting in a puddle of urine!**

4. He had to be photogenic – My years of attempting to get cute photos of all-black Anja made me envious of my friends with dogs you could actually see in pictures.

5. I thought a border collie mix would be nice. I didn't want to deal with the intensity of a full border collie but I thought it might be nice to have a dog who was pre-programmed to learn and interact with people.

6. He needed to be a male. No sense causing trouble with Kaddi. I need to pick my battles carefully and having Kaddi be gracious to a new female interloper in the house would not be one of them.

So what did I end up with? I call Charlie a *Condensed Borderless Collie* a very cute little black and white dog who knows no bounds. He'll try just about anything and sees every fence as a challenge to surmount. The part about wanting a puppy? I knew something was amiss as I watched my new potential adoptee lift his leg on every bush he could find. Oh well, he's part of the family now and we'll learn to live with his idiosyncrasies!

First Meeting - 9/18/2009

I met him for the first time today. I was scared that I'd like him and scared that I wouldn't. It's very hard to be careful enough in choosing a new companion for the next 10 – 15 years. Will he be the right fit, will he have the personality and zip to do what he will be expected to do? Last week, I made a wish list of characteristics I wanted in my next dog

So, today I drove a hundred miles to meet a cute fellow named Woodie. (Since I work with lots of teenage kids, that name was going to have to go. I hear it's a sexual slang term….) I found "Woodie" on Petfinder.com after narrowing down my search by looking for "border collie, baby, male" within driving distance of my home. I found the little guy in North Star Border Collie rescue and immediately emailed off a note to his foster Mom.

So my first impressions are good. Woodie is very cute, photogenic, very friendly and plays well with other dogs. On the down side, even though he's black and white, I don't think he's really a border collie mix. My age requirement also just went out the window too. I'm sure he's well over a year old. It appears by his obsessive marking behavior and well-developed reproductive organs that he wasn't neutered until he reached adulthood.

On the good side, he was very at ease with people and had good dog manners.

We practiced "walk-by's" with Reggie and Kaddi. Woodie was able to control himself on leash without lunging at my dogs. Within a few minutes, we had him sitting and taking treats within a few feet of Reggie and Kaddi. We did each dog separately. Kaddi was calm near him and not aggressive meaning she wasn't scared of him. She can look like "Cujo" when she's threatened. Some dogs just make her uneasy and reactive. Her behavior today was very promising.

We took Reggie and Woodie down to the fenced play yard and unhooked their leashes. Both continued to be at ease with each other and within a few minutes were playing a nice game of chase.

This all looked very promising. I do have a few reservations however. Will Woodie ever be the kind of dog I can have off leash for a walk in the woods? He looks awfully drawn to the scents in the forest. In the large pen, he wandered around oblivious to our presence and didn't respond at all to our calls. His obsessive leg lifting was turning me off. Also the car ride and new environment had stressed him as his normally firm poops had turned to diarrhea.

Woodie's foster parents, Carole and Ken, have been doting over this little guy. They've already been training him with the eye contact game and Ken has been taking him on numerous long walks. One thing I asked them to change was to no longer play hand-grabbing games with him. I've found that's a good way to make a snappy, defensive dog. No more chasing him around the house either. No sense making a dog who's good at running away from people.

We also looked more closely at his body shape trying to guess his breed heritage. He's definitely not shaped like a border collie, his body is a bit broad and chunky with no tummy tuck and hooked tail. He's mighty cute, but that new fur that's growing in seems coarse and maybe, terrier-like.

So, weighing all the positives and negatives, this little guy is already worming his way into my heart. As I look at his photos I see a sparkle in his eyes and a willingness to communicate with people. I said "yes" to having this little guy come into our family.

Moments after our first meeting, Charlie has already learned that sitting calmly earns him treats!

Kaddi gets her first sniff of her new brother - very carefully!

2
CHOOSING THE DOG OF YOUR DREAMS
OR THE DOG OF YOUR NIGHTMARES!

Often, we don't really choose our dog pets. They just happen to us. The sad stray grabs our heartstrings as we walk through the humane society kennels, or an appealing waif needs a home because his owners can no longer keep him.

But what if you actually took the time and energy to research the breed or type of mix you wanted to bring into your home for the next decade or so? What variables would you want to control?

Age: If you choose a **young puppy**, you'll have the joy of nurturing the little fellow and watching him grow. You'll be able to train him and head off behavior problems before they become habits. The flip side is you'll have months, even a year, before this little guy will be reliable out of your field of vision. You'll have the joy of cleaning up lots of "accidents" and, most likely, will have a few valued items destroyed by his teeth along the way.

An **older puppy** will require fewer months of direct monitoring, fewer accidents, and, if you're lucky, you'll have fewer mangled belongings.

An **adolescent dog** in a shelter usually means that the last owners have already thrown up their hands in despair because they didn't ever get around to training their pup and now can't stand his obnoxious behavior.

A **young adult** might be nice since he's outgrown the puppy crazies or maybe his human parents just tolerated his bad behavior a bit longer than the parents who turned in their dog as an adolescent. This could be a great find if the dog has been trained a bit and is used to being part of a human family. This dog will be lots of work if he's already been rewarded for unacceptable behavior.

An **older adult** will be a great companion if he's been raised with consistent positive training. Unfortunately there are lots of people out there who have no concept of what that means. Your new dog companion may have learned to be sneaky if his former parents yelled at him to try to change his behavior. He may have learned that other dogs are scary, when they allowed other dogs to bully him, or maybe they used an electronic shocking containment system and now he thinks that running up to greet passersby and little kids causes a shocking experience. He's now aggressive and fearful of anyone new he sees.

Breed Type: Remember up until a hundred years or so ago, most dogs had jobs and their breed types reflected their abilities to do those jobs well. In other words, don't get a collie and expect it to not bark or a border collie and expect it to not herd. Stay away from hounds if the sound of baying drives you crazy and terriers if you don't want pieces of dead stuffed toys strewn around your house. Do your homework and research the activity levels and gifts of different breeds.

Personality and Sensitivities: If the previous owners gave up their dog because he was eating through walls every time there was a thunderstorm, don't expect this guy to magically transform when you own him. Fearful dogs tend to remain fearful dogs. You can spend years desensitizing them but, in a new scary situation, they'll most likely still be fearful dogs! Often, however, wild and crazy dogs are just unfocused and untrained. There's lots of hope for those guys with good training and outlets for their energy.

Watch out for people talking about dogs with "alpha" personalities or "dominance" issues. Dogs that are grumpy or growly have usually learned the behavior because it has worked to protect them from scary situations. If a dog already has a history of using his teeth to communicate with people, this could land you in a lawsuit someday when he grabs the wrong person. Don't assume that your love and caring can cure him of his aggression. You'll need to learn to manage this guy so he doesn't ever get into a situation that will cause him to bite someone.

> If you'd like to see lots of choices for dogs to adopt go to www.PetFinder.com

---

Waiting for a New Friend - 9/25/2009

I'm getting excited about having a new friend come to our house. We won't welcome him here until we return from being away next week. There's no sense bringing the little guy here and then immediately leaving town. That would be confusing for him. Besides, I want to be here to monitor his behavior with our current dogs. First impressions are so important!

My rescue friends have agreed that we better check out his obsessive peeing. His foster parents say they've never met a dog that drinks so much and pees so much. I'm concerned that he may have unresolved health issues, perhaps a UTI, crystals in his bladder, diabetes or kidney or liver problems.

His foster family has been feeding him an exceptionally high protein food. They'll be gradually switching him to a proven holistic food before he comes here.

3
WELCOMING A NEW DOG INTO YOUR FAMILY

Imagine traveling to a foreign country where you had no understanding of the language or no knowledge of the local customs. What if some of the things you liked to wear, eat or do were considered totally inappropriate in the culture of this foreign land?

Now think of what it's like to a pup or even an older dog when you bring him into your home. He doesn't know anything about your family, your likes and dislikes, and not only that, in his doggy culture, ripping things apart, digging holes and peeing to mark his territory are completely normal.

Your job as this pup's new guardian is to help him feel safe while managing his behavioral options so he doesn't have a chance to get himself into situations that you can't stand.

Before your pup comes home, you need a plan to make his transition into your family a positive experience. The last thing you want to do is to allow him to get into situations that are going to have him feel unsafe in his new environment.

Some things to think about before you bring the pup home

Before you bring the pup into your house, have a family meeting to figure out just what you're going to do with this little fellow. Where's he going to be staying at night while you sleep, and during the day when you can't watch him? Who's going to exercise him and let him out to relieve himself when you're not there to be with him? Where's he going to relieve himself outside and how are you going to manage him while he's doing that? Dog trainers have a formula they use to help clients get an idea of how often their pup is going to need to go outside. Take the age of the dog in months and add one to get an idea of how long a pup can most likely go between potty breaks. So, for example, if your pup is three months old, 3 + 1 = 4 or four hours maximum time without urinating or defecating. So, who's going to be your puppy godmother who's going to let him outside when you can't be there? Or, are you going to puppy-proof a room in your house and expect him to relieve himself on doggie potty pads?

Some people think that confining a pup is cruel and insist that letting the pup loose in their house while they're not available is the way to go. This is both dangerous to your pup (Who knows what part of your furniture he'll ingest while you're away?) and very dangerous to your belongings. Besides, our goal is to have a dog friend who feels safe with us. If we come home and turn into raging idiots when we find our pup's been eating the drapes while we're away, he's for sure going to think he's landed on the planet with a bunch of psychotic primates.

First Greeting

First impressions are of the upmost importance. How is he going to be introduced to your human family members and other pets? Is he going to feel safe, or scared and overwhelmed in his new environment?

Whether your new pet is bold or timid, his first introductions with your family need to be done with a bit of preparation. Wouldn't you rather hang out with a new acquaintance who greeted you with a bouquet of flowers than one who dumped a bucket of cold water on your head at your first meeting?

You'll want to have some very good treats on hand for that first "handshake." Make that first meeting the first training session with your new friend. You'll most likely be doing this greeting at the rescue facility where you're picking him up or at the breeder's home.

Check out the detailed description of the *Don't Eat the Hand That Feeds You* (Chapter 5) game. Very simply, you'll hold an extremely enticing food reward rolled up in the palm of your hand. Hold your hand out and let the pup sniff your hand. Stay calm as he attempts to get the food by nuzzling, clawing, chewing or drooling on your hand. The first second he stops the obnoxious behavior, say "yes," open your hand and give him the yummy. Repeat this until he catches on that the treat is available to him when he stops acting like a drooling fool and calms himself to receive the food. Within five minutes or so, he'll figure this out, especially if your timing is good and you say "yes" the second he removes his attention from the food.

Reggie "reacquaints" himself with Charlie before the drive back to our house

You can immediately move into the *Eye Contact* (Chapter 5) game, now that your pup is not accosting you for the food. Wait until he glances your way before saying "yes" and opening your hand and reward him for looking at you for a brief second. In just a few minutes, he'll catch on, if your timing is accurate.

Usually, by this time he may already be sitting, looking at you, to get the treat. If not, you can help him learn his new trick by luring him into a "sit position." Hold your tidbit-filled hand just above his head and then move it back across his body. His back legs will automatically fold down, and your pup will be sitting.

Play this new "sit and look at me game" with each family member. Help your toddlers by folding your hand around theirs while they hold the treat. Even three-year-olds can be great at saying "yes" with you to mark the nice calm non-hand-eating behavior of the pup.

You'll want do this whole procedure with the pup on a leash to prevent him from bouncing off your kids or careening through your house instead of being focused on learning his new trick.

Meeting the Rest of Your Dog Family

How your new pup meets the resident dogs is going to determine whether you'll have a happy dog family for years to come. Introducing your pup to your current dogs must be done carefully so everyone feels safe, both your new pup and your seasoned dog friends.

You'll want to read the section, *What is a "Walk-By,"* (Chapter 4) before you even think of letting your resident dogs meet the new pup. Remember: ***first impressions are extremely important!***

Imagine, you're sitting in your easy chair when a stranger bursts into your home, smacks you around a bit, proceeds to empty your refrigerator and then zonks out on your bed telling you to buzz off when you try to enter your own bedroom! Can you imagine what your dog friends would feel like if you let your new pup barge into your home, attack their bodies with his puppy teeth, empty their food bowls and then move into their beds?

Remember, your job as a good pet manager is to have all of your dogs feel safe in your home. You don't want your resident dogs to charge up and scare your new pup nor have the new pup barge into their space.

Set up your new pup's crate away from your current dog's eating and sleeping areas. Drape the crate with a blanket or sheet on three sides so the new pup will have a safe corner. When you bring the new pup into the house for the first time, stick the resident dogs in the back bedroom for a while so there's no way they'll have a chance to overwhelm the newcomer. If they're intimidating barkers, stash them even farther way or give them a chewy to keep them occupied for a while.

First, put the new pup on a long line and take him for a leisurely walk around your yard. Don't walk him near any windows where your confined resident dogs can see him and terrify him with their barking. Even if your yard is fenced, keep him on a line. He's going to be using that line until you get a chance to teach him a very reliable recall. He'll probably relieve himself during that walk. Next, bring the new dog into the house on a leash and let him explore a bit. Practice his new sitting and eye-contact tricks in a few different areas. Put him into his new crate for a second or two and let him back out. Repeat this a few times rewarding him for doing his new sit and eye contact games in his crate. In the future, this will be required behavior each time he's released from the crate. If he's jumping around like a ninny and you open the crate door, he'll be learning to act like a wild and crazy animal to get you to open his crate door.

Now it's time to start doing "walk-bys" with your other dogs. Take your time and follow the "walk-by" procedure with each of your other dogs. If your dogs tend to be reactive, start at a distance far enough away so they won't react or bark. You might need to go to "neutral" territory, perhaps a park near your home rather than in your own yard. Your goal is to keep both your current dogs and the newcomer feeling

safe. You don't want any dog to get a chance to pounce on, blindside, or in any way intimidate another dog. Start out with the dogs far enough apart so you can keep them focused enough to take food rewards from you and not lunge or bark at the other dog.

Once you have the dogs able to take treats sitting near each other, it's time to take a leisurely walk with the two dogs, each being held by a different handler. At this point you're expecting calm relaxed behavior from both.

You'll have to judge for yourself when the dogs are comfortable enough with each other to interact more freely. Watch their bodies for signs of mounting tension. Make sure you have a drag line on each dog so you can call them away from each other before they get into tense aggression-provoking behavior.

Lacey and Charlie play with each other for the first time. Notice that Charlie is wearing a drag line so I can practice calling him away from play.

Be on the safe side if any dog has a history of becoming reactive when scared. I put a soft nylon muzzle on my Kaddi dog so she can't even think of using her teeth if she becomes overwhelmed when she meets a new dog. That way, I don't act scared worrying about what she might do.

Can't my dogs just "work it out on their own"?

I've heard so many people refer to their dog family as a "pack." You won't ever hear me use that term when referring to the collection of dogs that lives here.

For many people, a pack implies that there are "Alphas" and underlings, those with power and those without. They assume that it's natural and normal to have their family dogs picking on each other. Would you like to be the poor pup who lives in fear of the wrath of his housemates?

My job, as the keeper of my pet dogs, is to assure that each dog feels safe in our home. That means that no one is allowed to make someone else's life uncomfortable through intimidation.

Now this is a tricky undertaking. All animals are made to survive by testing their environment and finding the most rewarding ways to get what they need. They do what works for them and they get better at doing those things through practice.

So, what if one of my dogs learns that growling at the other dogs scares them away from me? I've had lots of people tell me that one of their dogs is "jealous" of their other dogs and won't let them come near to get treats or affection. What do you suppose happens if the owner allows this grumpy bullying to work? You guessed right – the intensity of the bullying increases since the behavior has worked for the dog.

Can you see what the long-term ramifications of allowing a dog to be rewarded by bullying means for peace in your canine family?

Be very careful if you have a multiple dog family. Play should be fun with no dog being bullied by another.

My job is to protect the safety of each dog in my family. When a new dog visits our house, or when I'm introducing a new dog into the family, it's my job to have the experience be rewarding to all of the dogs. I can't let any dog be picked on, scared, or allowed to steal resources from another.

We always do "walk-bys" when first introducing a new dog, so that the dogs can get a chance to meet each other without becoming scared. We don't ever just put them together and "let them work things out."

Some things to do to keep your dog family life peaceful:

❖ The new dog should be safely crated when you're not there to monitor interactions with the rest of the dog family. The crate should be away from the area of the other dogs. Can you imagine how intimidating it would be if you were the new dog, stuck in a crate, while a dog like Kaddi made "evil eyes" at you? If nothing else, drape three sides of the crate with a sheet so the new dog will feel safer.

❖ Monitor all dog interactions, inside and out of doors.

❖ Practice calling the dogs away from each other and rewarding them. You may need to keep a drag line on at least the new dog to be able to gently help him come to you.

❖ Call the dogs away before the play gets rough. Don't tolerate any bullying play, where one dog looks like he's running for his life, or dogs are playing "let's all pile on another dog."

❖ Watch the dogs' eyes and call them away from staring at each other.

❖ If your new dog is an obnoxious puppy, limit the time he can spend harassing your other dogs. You don't want your older dogs to have to hide from him or get snarly to protect themselves from his piercing puppy teeth.

❖ Make the presence of the new dog very rewarding to the rest of your dog family. Call them all over and have them sit for cookies near each other. The more they're all together being calm, the more cookies they get to share!

In time, you will have a peaceful family with no bullies and no one feeling bullied, a safe place for all your dog companions!

4
WHAT IS A "WALK BY"?

Doing dog-dog introduction in a safe way for all...

How do you act when you're introduced to a new person? Be aware next time when you greet a new acquaintance. You make brief eye contact; shake the person's hand while exchanging pleasantries, and then take a step back from the person you've just greeted. Now, what would you think, if you went to shake hands with a new person and the guy grabbed you and twisted your arm behind your back into a hammer lock? Or what if you started to shake hands and, suddenly, this stranger grabbed you and started groping you all over your body. I assume you might be offended.

How many times have you seen people let their dogs charge up to a strange dog and do just about the same thing?

I'm amazed when I see how many people have their dogs greet each other for the first time. People will let their dogs lunge at another dog, bouncing and gagging, and then let their dog either mount the other dog, or shove his nose in the other dog's butt. Gosh, that's impolite!

At Dog Scout Camp, we've come up with a formula that works consistently well for having our dogs greet each other. Our goal is to have the dogs meet without either one having to get grumpy or defensive and lash out at the other dog, thereby ruining the trust that the two might have had in each other.

We call this greeting process "doing walk-bys." We let the dogs get a chance to see that the other dog is not going to blindside them by charging up to them and jumping on them or attacking them.

We start with the owners and their dogs about forty feet apart. Ideally, the dogs are on front-attached harnesses so they'll be easy to turn and less stressed by not having pressure on their throats. (Imagine doing a relaxed handshake while someone is throttling your throat!) The owners each have yummy treats in their hands.

We have the owners and dogs walk past each other at increasingly closer distances. We start with the dogs on the outside of their owners. The two owners walk toward each other but pass each other at least twenty feet apart. They will encourage their dogs verbally while walking, and, if necessary, lead them with a treat as they pass the other dog. The goal is to have the two dogs pass each other with neither of them becoming aroused.

Kaddi demonstrates the "Walk-By" procedure at Dog Scout Camp. She can be very fearful of dogs she doesn't know. Doing a walk-by assures her that the other dog won't hurt her.

The owners then turn and repeat the process of walking past each other, always encouraging their dogs. When the dogs can pass each other and remain relaxed, the owners decrease the distance from each other when they pass.

Once the dogs can walk past each other and remain relaxed, we repeat the process, this time with the dogs on the inside so they'll pass each other not separated by their owners. We want the dogs to be at least about ten feet apart the first time they pass. We do this a few more times at a closer distance.

If you watch each dog closely while you're doing this, you'll see that the dogs are starting to check each other out with little glances, or maybe a little appeasing tongue flick. What you want to guard against is having either of the dogs locking onto the other with his eyes or displaying other threatening behavior. If necessary, have the owner lead the dog with the offensive behavior with a treat under his nose. If either dog is too aroused to walk by without getting upset, you need to back up the process and move the dogs and people farther apart.

Finally, the dogs are now close enough as we pass to turn their heads and catch a sniff of each other as they pass. During the next pass, we slow a bit more to let them get another sniff. And finally, we let them stop and do a quick "handshake," a sniff of about two seconds.

Kaddi is now closer to the other dog and checking him out by taking a quick sniff.

We've done walk-bys with hundreds of dogs at Dog Scout Camp. Over the years, we've come to the realization that what most people consider normal dog greeting can set the dogs up to become reactive with other dogs. Dogs learn to perform "preemptive strikes," to be the one who bullies the other dog before the other dog gets a chance to bully him. Imagine, if every time you met a new acquaintance you had no idea whether that person was going to grab you. Wouldn't you learn to grab her first? That's what countless ill-informed people have let go on between dogs that are meeting for the first time. Their dogs learn to protect themselves by either grabbing another dog first or learning to grovel to appease the aggression of another dog.

By getting our dogs used to these careful greetings, our dogs become less reactive when meeting new dogs. They trust us to keep other dogs from being impolite with them so they don't have to be snarly when another dog approaches.

Brenda Aloff is the friend and trainer who first introduced me to the art of doing "walk bys." Her book *Canine Body Language* is a great resource. You can see Kaddi doing more walk bys at Dog Scout Camp.

Woodie 10/6/2009

Woodie is here and sleeping peacefully in his crate. My neighbor Therri, my big Tervuren Reggie and I met Woodie and his foster Mom in a motel parking lot about 30 miles away just a few hours ago. He recognized Reggie and me and immediately curled up in his dog bed on the seat of the car and went to sleep next to Reggie.

On the way home Therri and I stopped at Staples to buy a new point and shoot camera since my old one has been acting unreliable. We tried buying at Best Buy but were chased out of the store by an army of sales people who were incensed that we'd brought a dog in with us. I sure wasn't going to leave the little guy alone in my car. Staples was much friendlier and made some money from our visit. Woodie was good in the store and looked like he'd like to drag us around to meet everyone he saw. He seemed to become whiny and impatient easily.

When we got home, we put him on a long line and let him wander around the yard. He sure does like to pee on things. Since he was just neutered a couple of months ago, I'm hoping this behavior will decrease somewhat over time. He started barking wildly when he saw Bluebell the goat but settled down after a couple of minutes.

Once he'd had chance to wander a bit, we brought Lacey outside and did "walk-bys." She relaxed after a few minutes and we unhooked her leash and let her wander loose. We did the same with Kaddi. I put a nylon muzzle on her when we released her since I've watched her bite two dogs in the butt that intruded on our yard in the last few years. She will wear that when loose near him until I'm sure she's no longer scared of him.

He was noisy, making gross screaming-barking noises when I first put him in his crate but settled down within a couple of minutes.

My assessment so far:

- ❖ Woodie seems very confident in a number of situations.

- ❖ He has great dog language with his peers.

- ❖ He has no concept of coming to his name.

- ❖ When given freedom to roam on a long line he wanders without checking in on people.

- ❖ He pulls like a maniac on a leash with no awareness of the person holding it. He should be great at pulling my dog sled.

- ❖ He rides well in the car but tends to spin and tangle himself in his harness as he settles down.

- ❖ He's an experienced gate opener – as soon as he saw the gate at the end of the driveway, he tried to nose his way through.

- ❖ He does a beautiful sit with eye contact to get a cookie but tends to often bounce off people before the sit.

My training goals for the day

- ❖ The name game

- ❖ Come game

Wolf or "Woof"

Some Thoughts on Letting Go of the Dominance Paradigm in Training Dogs

"You've got to show your dogs who's boss. To be a good dog trainer, the owner must be Alpha. The problem with your dog is that he's too dominant."

If you read dog-training books, watch popular TV or hang around with dog people, you are bound to come across statements like these. Somehow, people have decided that being the "top wolf" to your dog is going to make him a better pet or solve training problems. If you could just put the dog "in his place" he would be obedient and listen to your "commands."

I have found that using the dominance paradigm in training dogs is counter-productive.

Let me elaborate some of my thoughts:

❖ **Comparing Assertive behavior of adult breeding wolves to dog training is ludicrous.** "Alpha" wolves (now called "breeders" by most wolf biologists) do not train other members of the pack. Current wolf studies have also shown that they are not always the leading animals when wolves travel, nor do they always lead in hunting or eat first when a kill is made.

❖ **Even "wolf people" stay away from the wolf paradigm when dealing with human socialized wolves.** Many years ago, when I became a wolf educator, most of us dealing with socialized wolves believed that we needed to act like wolves to interact with them. From the time the wolves were pups, we handled the "social climbing" animals with vigilance, aware that we must be "dominant" for them to remain "submissive."

Beth and an old wolf commune at Wolf Park on a very cold day. The staff at Wolf Park are very skilled at handling wolves in cooperative rather than dominance based ways.

Unfortunately, this method of handling wolves backfired on many of those who used it. When humans attempted to interact with these socialized wolves in this way, the wolves were more apt to challenge and hurt the humans when the wolves reached sexual maturity.

❖ At Wolf Park, a wolf education and research facility in Battle Ground, Indiana, the staff has learned that careful, non-confrontational, behavioral shaping methods work best in dealing with the wolves. The staff members do not attempt to act like wolves when interacting with them.

❖ **The dominance paradigm assumes that a socially repressed dog will be an "obedient" dog**. Dogs learn by exploring their environment and repeating behaviors that are rewarding to them. Good trainers manage their dogs to prevent them from practicing unwanted behavior and to reward behavior that they want to foster. They do not attempt to suppress behavior through intimidation or force.

❖ **Dogs that are pushed around by their owners who are attempting to show them "who's boss" are more apt to redirect aggression to other humans and dogs.** If someone has been picking on you, you're more apt to take out your frustration on someone else.

❖ **Often a dog's body postures and behavior are labeled "dominant" when, in fact, the animal is really fearful or defensive.** Sadly, if a fearful or defensive dog is "corrected" by a misinformed trainer who is concerned about the dominance issue, the result will most likely be a dog that becomes even more fearful and defensive.

❖ **Working with a dog using the dominance paradigm sets up the owner and the dog for a confrontational rather than cooperative relationship.** Good trainers don't let themselves get into "power struggles" with their dogs.

❖ **Diagnosing behavioral problems within the dominance paradigm leads to enacting policies with the dog that are useless and not apt to deal with the real training issues that need to be addressed.**

I am surprised that the dominance paradigm continues to flourish despite all the information that disputes its use. When we began working with Kaddi, the African village dog my daughter brought us from her village in The Gambia,

> Learn about wolves. Attend a wolf behavior workshop @ www.WolfPark.org

many of her less desirable behaviors could have been characterized as dominance related to those who choose to think in that mindset. Her gut reaction to any fearful situation was to charge, snarling with tail and hackles raised. She was an ardent resource guarder who seemed to go out of her way to try to stare down our other dogs. I don't know how many misguided dog people told me she was a "dominant bitch" and I should be correcting her and lowering her social status. I chose to prove them wrong. I suspected that Kaddi was just fearful in many situations so I continued a careful socialization program with her. For many months, she was hand fed, kibble by kibble, practicing eye contact and other operant behaviors. We intervened by luring her away from stare-downs with our dogs and rewarding her for choosing alternate behavior. She is now ten years old and doing wonderfully in all respects. She is very lucky that we chose to train rather than dominate her, and so are we.

Woodie 10-6-2009 – Part 2

I couldn't believe I did it! I managed to erase all of the photos I took on my new little camera so I invited Therri back over to take some more. So much for getting pictures of the dogs looking scared of each other!. My guys and Woodie were relaxed without being fearful. We kept the nylon muzzle on Kaddi just to be sure.

We decided to start working on Woodie's recall and new name recognition. We started by standing in one place and saying his new name "Charlie" and giving him treats. We then took turns restraining him while one of us backed away after waving a cookie under his nose to get his attention and then calling his name. The person restraining him then released him so he could come to the caller and get the cookie.

He was doing so well that we started moving farther away to call him and added the "come" word to our call. We added the word "wait" as we walked from him since he couldn't come anyway as he was being held by the drag line on his harness. He liked this game so much that we started running off and hiding in the bushes before calling him. He charged toward us like a maniac and sat to get his cookie reward.

For the time being, we will only use his new name when we're training recalls or giving him cookies. When just petting him or hanging out, he'll still be Woodie for the time being; I don't want his new name to just become another meaningless word that he ignores.

Dear Woodie greeted Bob like a long-lost friend. Bob was pleased since every other dog we've ever adopted was afraid of him at first.

5
YOUR DOG'S BRAIN

Don't expect a deep scientific treatise here on canine cognition. I'll leave that work to some of my colleagues who are much more qualified than I to do deep scientific explanations. Instead, I'd like to use a metaphor that trainer Brenda Aloff stuck in my mind many years ago.

Check out this website if you are interested in finding out more about animal cognition
http://www.animalcognition.net/

Here is a picture of my dog Kaddi's brain:

Kaddi's Brain

You can clearly see two competing functions in her brain: there's the *Einstein* part and then Kaddi's *Lizard* brain.

I'll bet you've met lots of dogs who spend most of their time stuck in Lizard Brain. They're the ones you see lunging on the end of a leash trying to drag their owners up to every passing dog or interesting human. They're the ones who bark, bounce and gag at the end of their leashes. If a dog is stuck in Lizard Brain, he's apt to be impolite about grabbing food from your hand and will be just all around hyper. He's impulsive, reactive and unfocused.

Now, consider the dog who has practiced being a thinking dog. The Einstein function in his brain has been developed so he is better able to think rather than impulsively react. He knows how to keep himself calm in a variety of settings. He doesn't grab food impulsively, he can remain calm when in the presence of distractions and he is responsive to his owner's cues.

Does this sound impossible to you? Maybe you've never learned the tricks to help your dog develop his Einstein potential. This book will guide you through the process of helping your dog be the best thinking dog he can be!

The First Step – A Default Sit

Dogs, just like people, learn to do what works best for them to get what they want. They try different behaviors. The ones that work the best become the ones they use the most.

Many dogs learn that charging up to people and bouncing off their bodies is the best way to get people to interact with them. "How do I get my dog to stop jumping on people" is probably the most common lament heard by all dog trainers.

What if the behavior of jumping on people were replaced by a more socially acceptable behavior like approaching people and then calmly sitting in front of them?

We dog trainers are often asked how to "break" a dog of doing something. Instead we should be thinking of which behavior we'd like to teach to replace the unwanted behavior.

The easiest way to get rid of the "jumping on people" behavior is to teach a trick that is more rewarding to the dog; to teach the dog that the best way to get what he wants is to approach people and calmly sit in front of them. We call that a "default sit." That means that the dog will sit without being asked. It becomes an automatic thing he does when he walks or runs up to a person.

The easiest way to teach a sit is simply by holding a piece of food in your closed hand and then move your hand back over the head of your dog. The dog will follow the smell of the food and rock back onto his butt and into a seated position. The second his butt hits the floor, say "yes" and give him the treat. Do this a few times and he'll get the idea very quickly.

Now, take a few steps back and repeat the process, saying "yes" the second his butt hits the ground and then rewarding him.

Liam trains his Bull Mastiff puppy Buzz to do a default sit. Notice that Buzz is tethered to help prevent him from jumping on Liam while he practices his trick.

Now step back, skip the hand motion and wait until he figures out that the sit behavior that worked a few moments ago is the one that will work again to get a treat. Most dogs will immediately try the sit behavior.

Practice this new trick and he'll get better and better at it. Just remember, every time you don't practice this trick and instead reward your dog for jumping on you by petting or interacting with him, you'll be teaching him a different trick – one that can drive you and your friends crazy!

Default Sit for a Crazed, Obnoxious, Lizard Brained Dog

Yes, there are some dogs that are so hell-bent on jumping on people that they may not even notice your attempts to calm them into a sit position. I've met over-enthusiastic puppies who were so happy to see me that their brains no longer functioned. I met one beautiful husky pup who became extremely aroused when I attempted to work with him, grabbing and biting at my body. I found out later that his owner had been training him with a shock collar. I'll tell you more about the ill effects of punishment-based training later.

If you're finding that your pup is too bouncy to notice your food lure, there's a very simple management trick that can help you.

Put a harness on your dog and attach his leash to the ring on the top back position. Hook the end of the leash to an immovable object. You could loop it around the leg of a heavy piece of furniture or the base of a small tree. Just choose your attachment point wisely so you don't end up pulling a leg off your heirloom coffee table!

Back away from your hyperactive puppy. He will probably strain at the end of the leash bouncing like a rabid bunny.

Now, slowly approach him, but not so close that he can make contact to your body with his feet. Hold your food lure in your closed hand just out of reach and at the level of his head so he will strain against the tether but be in a standing position. Now you can move your hand containing the treat back over his head and lead him into a seated position. Remember to say "yes" the moment his butt hits the ground and then open your hand to give him the treat.

Repeat this sequence: back away, approach, lure the sit, "yes" and reward a few times until he sits right away when you lure him into position.

Now approach just out of his reach and wait for him to sit before rewarding him.

This tethering game is a wonderful game to practice with guests, especially kids. It allows them to interact with your dog and help to train him without worrying that the dog will jump on them. You'll keep him from practicing "mugging" people and he'll learn that the best way to get attention when he approaches someone is to perform a nice calm sit.

Two games to start turning your dog from a Lizard to an Einstein

You can play these games with any age dog. If you start these right away with your new pup, you'll be helping him become a calmer pet for the rest of his life. An older dog may still have a lot of his Lizard behavior but these games will set him onto a path of being ready to learn more.

Don't eat the hand that feeds you...

This game teaches the dog to take food rewards gently without grabbing, while practicing calming himself.

❖ Hold a food morsel in your hand; palm upright, with fingers curled around the food. Most puppies will try to eat the hand, scratch at it with their paws, etc.

❖ Ignore all of the dog's obnoxious behavior. Wait him out. Do not say anything to the dog.

❖ When the dog stops pawing, biting, etc. for even a moment, say the word "yes" and reward the dog with the food by unrolling the fingers, palm side up.

❖ Repeat this until the dog will remain calm without mugging you and will take the food politely without grabbing.

❖ Practice this daily until the dog shows no interest in mugging you for food.

❖ Have others, especially children, practice this game with the pup.

The Eye Contact Game adapted from Chris Bach's Third Way™

This game teaches the dog to focus on his owner making eye contact despite distractions in the environment. Eye contact becomes the "default" behavior when the dog is interacting with the owner. The dog practices calming himself.

> These two games were introduced to me by my good friend trainer Chris Bach. Chris offers training programs through her web site: http://www.trainthethirdway.com/

❖ Work with your pup in an area with minimal distractions

❖ Put a big smile on your face. Show the puppy a yummy treat. Typically, the puppy will stare at the treat. He's already learned not to lunge and grab at it from practicing the *Don't Eat the Hand that Feeds You* game.

❖ Move the treat away from the pup, off to the side. The pup will probably continue to stare at the treat. Don't do anything.

❖ The second the pup's focus leaves the food, for even for the tiniest moment, say the word "yes" and give the treat to the dog.

❖ Continue this sequence, gradually rewarding longer glances away from the food.

❖ Once the pup knows to look away from the food when it is presented, begin waiting for the pup to make eye contact before saying "yes" and rewarding the dog.

❖ Gradually reward for longer eye contact

❖ Show the food again. If the pup chooses to look at the food, do as above until the pup decides that looking at the food causes the food to disappear.

❖ Work until the dog no longer takes a few moments to glance back and forth between the food and you but immediately looks into your eyes.

Lauren is practicing an advanced version of the Eye Contact game with Buzz. She has a tuna cookie in each hand and Buzz is choosing to look at her rather than grab the cookies.

Now that your dog stares at you rather than the food treats, you're using to reward him, he'll learn much faster as he watches you for his training cues.

Chris Bach with Kaddi and Chris' Border Collie, Stunner. Kaddi thinks Stunner is very cute!

Woodie Goes to School -   10-7-09

Never take your brand new rescue into new situations too fast, right? Oh well, I had a school program to do with pre-vet high school students and didn't think it would be a good idea to leave Woodie home stuck in a crate. So I loaded up his crate and dog bed and took off with him and the other dogs. I took along a sheet so I could cover the crate and keep him in a quiet corner so he wouldn't be overwhelmed in the new environment.

I didn't need to worry about all that. Woodie acted as though he'd been doing school programs his whole life. I gave the kids two instructions.

1. Do not call him. I didn't want to ruin his recall by having kids call him in two directions at the same time.

2. If he climbs up your body or jumps on you, ignore him. Only pet him if he has four feet on the floor.

He enjoyed the day schmoozing with the kids and lying quietly on a mat while I was doing my PowerPoint presentation. I will have to watch his drinking and peeing schedule as he let loose with a torrent of urine all over the classroom floor as he was greeting kids mid-afternoon. (Yes, he did have an outside break just an hour before.)

As the day progressed his climbing on humans behavior decreased. He does have a fascination with streamers hanging off human bodies and tried to grab a long plastic strip that was hanging off one girl's body.

In the evening, Bob and I practiced some restrained recalls. This little guy runs faster than any dog I've ever seen!

I'm already tired of being dragged by him when he's on a leash so I started working on some "walk by me" training. I hooked a leash to the front ring of his harness and the ring on his collar and practiced pivoting him around to me and rewarding him. Then I led him with some food so he'd be next to my left side. I used the "click" of my clicker to mark the second he was in the right position. I then took a step and marked when he was next to me. I encouraged him verbally and then continued to take a few steps at a time with him next to me clicking and rewarding intermittently as he walked by my side. I dropped the leash and continued our new game. If he tried to jump on me or bolt away, I just stepped on the leash and then encouraged him back into position.

For the first time, Woodie, Lacey and Kaddi had a wild game of chase around the yard.

6
TREATS, FOOD & OTHER YUMMIES

Have you ever looked closely at the content labels of dog treats and food? There's a secret that many dog people have discovered. The better the food going into the front end of your dog, the more consistent and more compact the stuff coming out the rear end. Cheap nutrition equals gross poops. Besides as the caretaker of your dog, don't you want your dog to have the best nutrition possible?

Always read pet food labels carefully. Stay away from products containing corn, wheat and rye since those grains are most apt to be moldy and the toxins produced by the molds can be fatal to your dog. Ingredients like "meat meal" and "by products" contain gross things that you probably wouldn't want to feed anyone you really liked. Watch out for new fad diets as many of these haven't been tested scientifically to provide good long-term health for your dog. Foods that contain both pre- and pro-biotics will help your dog have a healthy gut and healthy stools.

I find that many of my clients are avid dog food label readers who carefully choose a food for their dog but then err horribly when they buy treats. Make sure you read the labels on treats. All those cute things that look like meat, bacon or sausages are full of sugar, dyes and preservatives. Many of the healthier looking treats are being imported from countries that probably don't care as much about the health of your pet as you do.

> My favorite food and treats are formulated by a holistic veterinarian friend, Dr. Jane Bicks. My dogs have had the most consistent poops ever on the main diet, and the Tasty Rewards Training Treats are healthy, non-greasy and can be broken into miniscule pieces.. Find these products at: www.SuperPetFood.biz

Just remember, if you're using food rewards to train your dog, you want those treats to have an additive effect to the dogs nutrition, not detract from it.

The size of the treat is also *very* important. If you're training a tiny dog, you're going to need to be especially careful about the amount of food he's receiving through treats. If your dog is a chow hound, you can probably just use part of his kibble dinner for training rewards.

Some ideas for treats:

- ❖ Store-bought treats made in the USA with healthy ingredients

- ❖ Cooked white meat chicken from non-antibiotic –raised chickens (Studies have shown that people eating chicken that's fed a diet laced with antibiotics are more apt to contract antibiotic resistant bacterial infections.)

- ❖ Tiny pieces of cooked beef

I'm not into using hotdogs for training although I know they're very popular with many trainers. Even the best non-nitrate ones are salty and greasy. Just remember, you don't want to upset your dog's gut when you train him.

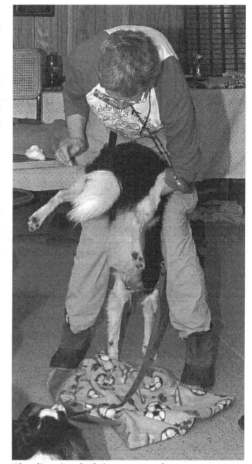

Charlie is helping me demonstrate a version of the Heimlich maneuver at Dog Scout Camp. This can be used if your dog gets a treat stuck in his throat. Use one arm to lift your dog's rear off the ground and then give him a tap with your other hand below his ribs.

Name Change! Woodie/Charlie - 10/9/09

What a smart little dog this guy is! He's a quick learner. Today we worked on:

❖ Down – I started by luring him down with a treat. After a few trials, I switched to leading him with my empty hand. Then I started adding the verbal cue "down" before my hand motion.

❖ Move into heel position – I did this in three steps. First I practiced getting him next to me by leading him with a treat and clicking and rewarding once he was in position next to me. Then I taught him to target (touch) my open hand by clicking and treating his approach and gentle touch. I was then able to lead him into the heel position with my hand with no food in it. Third, I practiced having him sit next to me. He learned to sit in front of his foster parents to get a treat. Now, I am getting him used to sitting in a new place relative to my body so I had to do the training position all over again, first luring, then without the lure and finally on verbal cue.

❖ Come – I let him wander loose in the yard and then called him with his new "Charlie" name. He came running like a mad man.

❖ Call away from the goat – I stayed close to him while he focused on dear Bluebell. He responded and came when I called. I then released him to bark again if he wanted by stepping away a bit and telling him to "go play."

❖ Call away from the other dogs – I waited until he was taking a breather from intense play and then called him. When he came, I rewarded him and then sent him back to "go play."

❖ Jump through a hula-hoop – Now that he knows how to hand target, it took only a few minutes to teach him how to jump through the hoop. He hesitated when I first brought it out. I clicked and treated him for being near it a few times before I started leading him through. I held the hoop touching the ground the first few times. And then raised it a few inches off the ground for him to jump through. I'll wait until he's really confident about this before I have him do any jump any higher.

I'm making a list of behaviors that I will not reward and hope to replace with behaviors I can stand.

- ❖ Barking at our dogs in the house – Both the dogs and I find this obnoxious. Reggie was sound asleep under the table when this little guy approached him and sat about a foot away barking in his face. I removed Charlie from the scene by dumping him back in his crate. In the future I will be more proactive and call him away from this behavior before it starts and reward him for an alternate behavior. Kaddi has been pretty tolerant of this guy but her patience is going to wear thin if he insists on doing this with her. Woodie is now wearing a drag cord when loose in the house so I can guide him away from these confrontations.

- ❖ Barking at the goat - Actually, I am tolerating this a bit. I'm going with him as he approaches the goat corral and using this as a practice time to call him away from barking.

- ❖ The hand grabbing is totally unacceptable. Unfortunately I know his foster Dad played this game with him quite a bit until he knew better. To counter this behavior, I'm just not getting involved when he tries to instigate it. I withdraw my hands and walk away. The body touching game will help him learn that remaining calm for approaching hands is a rewardable behavior.

- ❖ Scooting away from being handled, grabbed or restrained. I'm just not going to allow this behavior to happen. Both inside and outside he is wearing a drag cord attached to the back ring of his harness. I can easily step on it before I reach for him so he's unable to do the hop away trick. I can then reward him for sitting or standing quietly.

- ❖ Tugging at items in human hands – Rather than trying to stop him from doing the grabbing thing, I'm turning this into a fun but orderly game. I take a cloth toy (no socks!), let him tug a bit and then stop my tugging hand motion at the same time that I stuff a goodie into the corner of his mouth. He releases the toy. I then have him sit before I ask him to "get it" or throw the toy. He is doing very well at this. I am starting to add the cues "thank you" and "let go" as I remove the toy from his mouth.

- ❖ Looking for things to bark at – twice I've caught him staring out the back door making little growly sounds. I'd rather keep this behavior by happening by calling him away and rewarding him for alternate behavior

- ❖ Stealing stuff to run away and chew on it – I'll nip this behavior in the bud by working on the *Bad Dog Retrieve*. I'm keeping a drag line on him in the house so I can step on it and gently bring him back to me with the stolen goods and then reward him. He took off with a pen. I reeled him in, rewarded him and then tossed the pen a few times for him to retrieve. He lost interest after a few throws. He thought it was much more fun to eat the pen if it was a stolen object!

- ❖ Trying to dart out of open car doors – Charlie will be restrained in the car at all times. We will soon start practicing "wait" until released from the car

I'm also starting to see the side of his personality that probably got him into the rescue.

- ❖ Hand grabbing

- ❖ Sock grabbing – he thinks any cloth in a human hand is a tug toy

- ❖ Grabbing items and sneaking away with them to chew them up

Bluebell the goat finds dogs a fun challenge to torment. She wasn't intimidated by Charlie's barking

Charlie learns to jump through a hula-hoop using hand targeting

Luigi Cornyn Kotnik
10 months old

,

"In this picture, Luigi follows a simple "sit" command. Beth helped us start working with Luigi the day we brought him home at 12 weeks old. Using simple commands early on allowed Luigi to quickly understand what was expected during training sessions and has made him a very easy dog to work with."

The Kotnik Family

7
EQUIPMENT, TRAINING TOOLS AND YOUR DOG'S ATTIRE

You don't need a lot of fancy equipment to have a happy, well-trained dog, but the equipment you choose is going to play a large part in the effectiveness of your training. You'll want to use equipment that helps manage your dog while you're training him without scaring him or hurting him.

Can the use of the wrong equipment hamper your dog's learning? You bet it can! Take just a moment to put your hand on your own throat. Now apply some gentle pressure. Are you feeling a bit uncomfortable? Now imagine trying to fill out your IRS forms with that pressure on your throat. Do you get the picture?

When people attempt to train their dogs using equipment that makes the dog feel uncomfortable or even hurts them, they are hampering their dog's ability to think and learn. Many common dog training tools are aversive; that means their effectiveness depends on modifying the dog's behavior by doing something to the dog that the dog doesn't like. My dogs are my friends. Why would I ever want to use something that hurts or scares them to help them learn?

So, please forget your friends' advice to buy the latest training collar that is guaranteed to "show the dog who's boss," has teeth on it to "mimic a mother dog's correcting bite" or uses "just a little" static shock. None of those devices are going to help you build a better relationship with your dog. You want to choose equipment that is going to help the dog learn, not scare him into submission.

I'll tell you about my favorite equipment choices for training my dogs and how I use them. You may find something that works better for you. Just remember, anything that makes your dog more uncomfortable is likely to make his brain less available for learning.

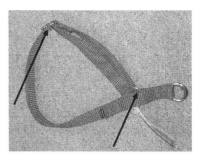

This collar is very adjustable and only tightens on the dog's neck a little bit

The Limited Slip Collar

Have you ever had the experience of having your dog slip out of his collar? There's nothing quite like standing helplessly, holding an empty collar, as your dog scampers away from you. To prevent this from happening, my favorite collar for my dogs is the type of collar my friends with sled dogs use. It's called a "limited slip" collar; that means it tightens slightly when a leash is attached to it. The collar doesn't pinch your dog's neck like a "choke" or training collar, but can prevent your dog from slipping away. There are similar collars that are called "martingale" collars, although they tend to tighten quite a bit more than the limited slip collars, and may put more pressure on the dog's neck than is comfortable. The only problem with limited slip collars is that they're hard to find in pet stores, whereas most stores carry martingale collars. It's worth sending away for one if you can't find one locally.

Here's a site where you can find very reasonably priced limited slip collars. Just beware, they sell sledding supplies too. You just may end up with a new winter pastime!
http://www.blackicedogsledding.com

A Harness with Chest and Back Leash Attachment Rings

My favorite training device for dogs is a harness with both a back and a chest ring for attaching a leash. Remember, I talked about using a tether to restrain your dog while teaching a default sit, having your dog automatically sit when a person approaches? You certainly wouldn't want to have your dog gagging, attached by his collar, to do that activity, so it's very nice to have a harness with a back attachment for some training activities.

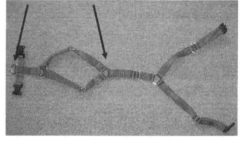

The "Sure-Fit" harness has both a chest and back ring where the leash can be attached.

Kaddi smiling in her favorite harness

My dog Kaddi taught me about using a harness rather than a collar for loose-leash walking. We were in Vermont where I was teaching at Camp Gone-to-the-Dogs. When I wasn't teaching, I was enjoying being a camper, trying to cram in as many classes as I could. I was hurrying, trying to walk both Kaddi and Anja from one activity to another. Kaddi had a harness on but her leash was attached to her collar. She'd pull too much when I hooked her leash to the back ring on the harness since she was used to pulling like mad when biking and sledding.

I had an idea: what if I were to attach her leash to the front ring of her harness instead of the back ring? Actually, I kept the leash hooked to her collar, and just clipped onto the front chest ring too. The photos will help you understand this a bit better.

Kaddi immediately became a different dog. She stopped lunging forward and relaxed. It was only then, that I realized how much having collar pressure on her throat had raised her anxiety level and made it impossible for her to be a thinking "Einstein" dog when she was being walked on a leash.

A big advantage of having the leash attached at the dog's chest is that the dog will be turned back toward you if he tries to pull forward. You'll then have a chance to regain his attention, reward him and then help him walk next to you. We'll talk more about loose lease walking in another chapter.

The "Sure Fit" harness is available from Premier Pet Products at: http://www.premier.com/

Look closely and you'll see that the drag cord is connected to the front chest ring and the collar ring to help swivel Kaddi back toward me if she pulls forward.

Since I started using Kaddi's harness with a front attachment almost a decade ago, other trainers and equipment suppliers have also caught on to using this design. There are now a number of front attach harnesses on the market. I've tried a few different models but still find the "Sure Fit™" harness made by Premier to be the most useful and comfortable of the designs. I'm leery of harness designs that are made to tighten on the dog's body if the dog pulls. Some harnesses tighten on the chest constricting the dog's shoulder when he pulls and I've seen others that seem to pull on the dog's armpits. I'd rather not use a piece of equipment that is designed to make a dog uncomfortable to get him to respond.

A Drag Line

Puppies and newly rescued dogs have a way of going places and getting into things you'd rather keep them away from. The last thing you want to be teaching your dog is that you're a scary monster who charges at him screaming while grabbing at his body. Remember, your goal is to always be safe *not dangerous to your dog.* You need a way to be able to move him away from forbidden places gently, without pouncing on him. Having a 6-foot lightweight leash or a line dragging from his harness allows you to stop his movement away from you without frightening him. Perhaps he's just grabbed your most valuable slipper and is sneaking away to consume it behind the couch. You can

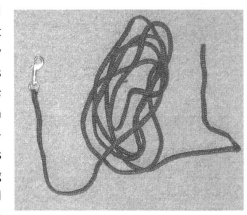

gently bring him back to you with his prize so you can practice *The Bad Dog Retrieve* described a bit later in this book.

A Long Line

We'll talk more about the use of long lines for training later. (see *The Glories of Using a Long Line*, Chapter 30) but for now, you'll want a long line (usually about 30 feet-long) to attach to your dog's harness when he goes outside. You never want him to learn that he's slippery and uncatchable when he's more than a leash-length away from you. These lines come in cotton or nylon of varying widths. Cotton will be easier on your hands.

I suggest having two long lines just in case you've not cleaned up the poop piles in your yard as efficiently as you'd hope to, and your pup manages to drag the thing through a wayward pile. You can always have a spare clean line for backup.

A variety of clickers

A Clicker

This is the little device that is going to speed up your training by "marking" your dog's behaviors that you're going to reward. You can get these at just about any pet store for a couple of dollars. I suggest you get more than one because they have a way of hiding themselves among household litter.

> For fancier clickers and lots of clicker training books and videos go to:
> www.ClickerTraining.com

Using a Head Halter as a Training Tool

Trainers who have adopted positive training methods often find leash pulling to be one of the hardest behaviors to retrain because, unfortunately, many dogs already have a long history of pulling on a leash and dragging their owner. This trained behavior has worked so well for the dog in the past that it's often hard to teach the dog a new way to respond to being walked on a leash.

Head halters provide an effective way to retrain a habitually pulling dog. A number of versions are now on the market, with the Halti™ and the Gentle Leader™ being the most common. Many trainers are strongly opinionated as to which design is best, but each works in a similar way, and all can be useful to retrain a pulling dog.

Head halters need to be introduced to the dog very carefully. Some early training methods suggested just putting the halter on the dog and letting him tough it out. The dog would buck and roll trying to get the thing off of his face. Most trainers now introduce the halter using lots of treats, getting the dog to be more accepting of this strange device.

Steps to introducing a head halter:

- ❖ With lots of good yummies in your hand, practice putting the dog's leash across his muzzle. Hold it there for a few seconds, treat the dog and then remove it.

- ❖ Work up to wrapping the leash around the muzzle for a longer period of time and reward the dog.

- ❖ Fit the neck loop of the halter around the dog's neck. Some instructions call for fitting this very tightly, although this is not necessary and may be more upsetting to the dog.

- ❖ Hold the loop of the halter open and offer the food treats through the loop.

- ❖ Continue to feed the dog through the loop moving the food farther away so that the dog must put his nose through the loop and put pressure against the loop to receive the food.

- ❖ Gently put the halter on the dog and continue rewarding the dog.

- ❖ Attach a leash to both the dog's collar and the halter. Continue to reward the dog.

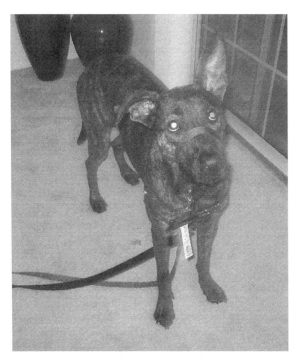

Emery showing off her new Gentle Leader™. This will help her practice turning her head away from dogs and passersby when out on walks. When she masters the skill of responding to slight pressure on her collar, she may no longer need to wear the Gentle Leader™.

- ❖ Start to walk slowly with the dog rewarding the dog when it chooses to not pull.

- ❖ The goal is to have the dog feel slight pressure on his neck collar before feeling the pressure on his nose. When the leash tightens on the neck collar, gently turn the dog's head to you by pulling slightly on the leash attached to the halter.

- ❖ The dog will learn to respond to the slight pressure on the neck collar. In most cases, the head halter can be eventually retired.

Almost a Week 10/12/09

The "Woodie" name is finally dead and gone! After practicing lots of recalls using his new name, Charlie, I finally feel secure in using his new name in other interactions with him.

Dear Charlie has been worming his way into our hearts and he's still been here less than a week.

Actually, I did curse him a couple of nights ago when he lifted his leg on the corner of our bed just as we were settling down to do some relaxed reading. I'm not sure what that was all about but we dumped him into his crate and vowed to watch him more closely in the future.

He'll be sleeping in his crate until we're sure he's past his marking behavior and long past his stealing and chewing games.

As I write, he's actually relaxed on the bed with me and Kaddi, a first time for this. Up until now, being on the bed has inspired chewing, grabbing, and wrestling behavior. I ignored his attempts to draw me into this game. Kaddi did some low but not too scary growls when he tried rolling on top of her. If the old behavior starts again, he'll go back into his crate. Somebody has obviously played obnoxious wrestling games with him on a bed. I'm hoping he'll learn he can stay up here as long as his behavior is calm and boring.

I just wiggled my leg and he immediately started chewing on it through the covers. When I moved a sheet, he started turning it into a tug toy. He's back in the crate for now until I have time to train and reward alternate behaviors. Bummer. By the way, "bummer" is my new "no reward marker." I'm saying that when he's earned his right to go back into the boring crate by being obnoxious.

His training is coming along. Bob and I worked on recalls - long distance and out of sight behind bushes in the yard. He's doing phenomenally well. We've been practicing hand targeting and using that to move him into heel position and leading him into jumping through a hoop.

I've been working to teach him "wait" (my preferred "stay" term). I helped him learn the concept by looping a long line around a post in the yard so that I could keep him from coming toward me. I'm also working on the "sit maintain" and "down maintain" exercises. He's catching on. I can now leave him, walk about 20 feet away and return while he stays in one place. I will be working to add distractions and longer time duration.

Charlie loves to play tug so I'm practicing having him tug on toys and then slipping a goodie into his mouth as I ask him to release the toy. I then have him sit before I have him "get it" and pull again.

I've started working on his retrieving behavior. He'll bring a ball or thrown toy to me and release it at my feet. At first, I did this on a long line so he didn't have the option of taking off with the toy and playing the "Na-na-na-na-na-you can't catch me" game. I would like him to have a very clean retrieve with him bringing an object to my hand and holding it until I ask him to release it so I'm going to have to do some organized training to get the results I want.

I started working in the house with him by giving him a pen since I know he has a predilection for wanting to steal pens and chew them up. I sat on the floor and offered the pen. When he grabbed it, I immediately said "yes" and removed it from his mouth and rewarded him. If he started chewing it, I just slid it quickly out of his mouth and did not reward him. After a few minutes, he was able to hold the pen gently without chewing. A bit later, I started substituting a retrieving dumbbell. While working with him, Kaddi, Reggie and Lacey took turns holding the dumbbell too. Of course they're pros at this. I was hoping that Charlie would catch on a bit faster by watching the other dogs get rewarded for calm holding behavior.

I did a few close dumbbell tosses and rewarded the other dogs for bringing back the dumbbell. Charlie did his first dumbbell retrieve!

Charlie learning to "wait" with the assistance of a long line looped around a post

Gracie

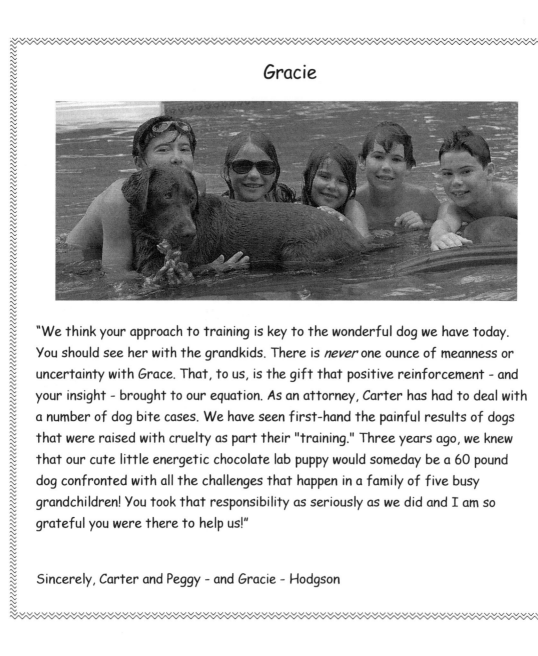

"We think your approach to training is key to the wonderful dog we have today.
You should see her with the grandkids. There is *never* one ounce of meanness or
uncertainty with Grace. That, to us, is the gift that positive reinforcement - and
your insight - brought to our equation. As an attorney, Carter has had to deal with
a number of dog bite cases. We have seen first-hand the painful results of dogs
that were raised with cruelty as part their "training." Three years ago, we knew
that our cute little energetic chocolate lab puppy would someday be a 60 pound
dog confronted with all the challenges that happen in a family of five busy
grandchildren! You took that responsibility as seriously as we did and I am so
grateful you were there to help us!"

Sincerely, Carter and Peggy - and Gracie - Hodgson

8
TAKING A PICTURE OF BEHAVIORS YOU LIKE

How does your dog know when he's doing something you'd like him to repeat?

What if you were sitting at work and your boss walked in and handed you a hundred dollar bonus. Wouldn't you be trying to guess what you did to earn it so you could repeat the behavior again to get another hundred?

Our dogs are like that too. They're always trying to make sense of their world to see if what they did before will produce the same gratifying results. If something works for them, they're more apt to repeat the behavior in the future.

Charlie with his favorite clicker

You can help your dog learn what behaviors you'd like him to repeat by using a **"Reward Marker."** It's like taking a picture of the behaviors you like and then rewarding them to get them to happen more often.

Many people say, "I just say 'good dog' and pat my dog on the head." Well, that may work a bit, but it's not all that efficient, and besides, many dogs aren't that fond of having their heads patted anyway.

To best communicate with your dog and teach him without confusing him, you're going to need a clear system to tell him which behaviors are worth repeating.

The best way to do this is to have a specific sound or signal that you can make the instant the dog is doing a behavior you like, and then give him a treat right away. The dog then has an idea of what behavior you're rewarding.

We're going to call this **"marking the behavior"** or a **"reward marker."** To be most efficient, you want to choose a marker that is something that will be unique to the dog and you'll use it only when you're specifically marking a behavior. It needs to be something that is quick and obvious to the dog.

Many dog trainers now use a **clicker**, a little noise maker you can hold in your hand. Something like that is most efficient because it's different from most other sounds the dog hears, is easy to use and, after a while, becomes a sound the dog loves to hear.

When I don't have a clicker handy, I'll also use a crisp cheery **"Yes!"** That works pretty well, but it's less obvious to my dog. I also must be careful not to be saying "yes" to him when I'm not about to reward him or the word will no longer predict that he'll be rewarded and my marker will lose its predictive power. "Good dog" just takes too long to say, and besides, I tell my dogs they're good just about anytime I'm hanging out with them. My marker needs to be unique and easy to notice so the dog will know the second he's doing a rewardable behavior.

Beware! Whatever behaviors you reward will be repeated! I had forgotten that I'd given treats to Charlie and Lacey for riding on the snow scoop last winter. That trick came back to haunt me the first snowfall this year!

Smartest Dog in the World! (When Not Peeing!) - 10/14/09

Charlie Darwin, the smartest dog in the world! Well, at least he's the smartest guy I've met in a while. He went back to the skill center with me yesterday to do programs on dog training for the pre-vet students. It's just been one week since he came to us and he's learning so fast he's already learning how to take money from people!!

One of my goals is to get him to be able to help with our annual Salvation Army bell-ringing project. Our dogs are trained to approach shoppers, look cute, then take their dollars, bring them back to us and stuff them in a bucket. To do that, the dogs need a number of skills:

- ❖ Dog can stand or sit in heel position

- ❖ Dog will approach another person on cue

- ❖ Dog will gently take a paper dollar from the person

- ❖ Dog will carry the dollar without chewing or ripping it

- ❖ Dog will bring the dollar to the handler

- ❖ Dog will drop the dollar into a bucket

Yesterday, Charlie carried his first dollar!

Charlie was a great demo dog except for when, after lunch, after he'd had a chance to take a break outside, he peed all over my lap while I was sitting and talking with the students!! Yuck! I couldn't believe what was happening as he stood there emptying his bladder on my pants! I'm not sure what's going on here since he wasn't marking – just plain letting loose all over the floor and me! As soon as he finished, he looked shut down. He turned away from me, tail between his legs and just stood there. I'm guessing he's been yelled at in the past for this behavior.

The kids and I just mopped up the floor and attempted to dry me off a bit. Nothing like continuing a program with urine soaked slacks!

Aside from this nasty surprise, Charlie was a gem all day. He did beautiful retrieves with the dumbbell, demonstrated moving into heel position and heeling, jumped my small agility jump with glee and cuddled with the kids.

Back at home, we played chase with the other dogs and even wrestled a bit with Kaddi.

I now feel comfortable letting him off his long-line and leash drag outside to play with our other dogs.

He's going to have his first bath in a couple minutes. He just came in covered with deer poop he's rolled in. Good thing I got him used to going in the bathtub a few days ago!

A very surprised urine-soaked Beth
Charlie must have been reprimanded harshly in his last home for his random peeing. Notice how's he's turned away from me and very sullen looking.

We made being in the bathtub a rewarding trick. When Charlie rolled in something disgusting outside, getting a bath wasn't a traumatic experience for him. You may notice that Charlie's coat looks different in later photos in this book. He had been shaved down at the shelter, probably because he came in covered with gross stinky stuff he loves to roll in so much!

9
HAND TARGETING

Hand targeting is a simple trick that will have many uses as you and your dog become working partners. The goal is to get your dog to move toward your open flat hand and touch it with his nose. This is a very simple trick to teach that will be handy for teaching many other behaviors.

Here are the beginning steps:

❖ Start with your dog sitting in front of you.

❖ Present your open flat hand a few inches away from your dog's face.

❖ He'll sniff your hand. Say "yes" or "click" and give him a treat.

❖ Do this a number of times, alternating which hand you present. Say "yes" or "click" your clicker the second his nose touches your hand.

❖ When you're pretty positive that he's going to touch your hand if you present it to him, add the verbal cue "touch" as you present your hand.

The next step is to get your dog to move his whole body toward your hand when you give the "touch" cue.

Beautiful Emery is learning to touch Stephanie's hand.

❖ Present your hand farther away from your dog so he has to get up from his sitting position to move toward your hand. Say "touch" and wait for him to get up and move toward your hand to touch it. Say "yes" or "click" each time his nose touches your hand.

❖ Now, alternate which hand you use and the distance you get the dog to move each time you give the "touch" cue.

❖ You should now be able to get your dog to move toward your hand, moving three or four feet to touch it.

Practice this trick in various different places in your house and outside in the yard. In the house, you could have him touch your hand to move your dog toward his dog bed. If he's on your bed and there's no room for you, have him hand-target to move toward a more acceptable location.

Touching your hand on cue will help you get your dog to focus on you when he becomes a lizard brain on walks (see *The Fine Art of Loose Leash Walking,* Chapter 26). Our Lacey dog worries a lot about the dog that lives in the yard at the end of our road. When we're driving up the road, she'll anticipate that she might see him and start breathing heavily when we're still a quarter mile away. If I extend my hand and have her touch it, she can bring herself back to Einstein brain and not work herself into a barking lizard.

Emery

"The touch command has proven very beneficial with my dog, Emery. She can easily become very excited and distracted and "touch" has taught her to re-focus her attention on me, allowing many high intensity situations to de-escalate."

Stephanie Thomas

More Pee....- 10/15/09

If only the peeing would stop...!

Charlie is doing so well!

He went to his first wolf program at the nature center. Before the kids came in I had him practice his new heeling trick and a few dumbbell retrieves. I'd rather build acceptable behavior from the start than try to fix obnoxious behavior later so I tethered him to a table leg to keep him from bouncing on top of the very young students when they came into the room.

He has a lot to learn about polite behavior with kids. In the few minutes he was loose, he greeted the kids effusively but for now, he'll be practicing calm tethered behavior during programs.

When the wolf program was done, I had the kids spread out around the edges of the room. Charlie was able to do his new tricks despite the distraction of thirty wiggling kids and their parents.

I've got a training program at the library next week and I had dog training flyers to pass out in town. I sure wasn't going to leave this cute guy in my car for a half an hour so I took him with me as I walked the main drag in town visiting the small shops to give them a flyer to post. Charlie did better than expected; imperfect leash walking but not crazed, friendly visits with a few store keepers and, luckily, no peeing!

I was hoping yesterday's pee bath was a fluke. Not so! He saved that for later in the day when I visited my dog training friends at their doggie daycare. Something is wrong with this pup! He was standing quietly between my friend April's legs when, to our shock, he let loose a deluge of urine all over the floor!

10
INTRODUCING NEW EQUIPMENT AND CLOTHES TO YOUR DOG

You've seen those dogs dressed as Santas or wearing felt antlers at Christmas time, or the pitiful little guys who've been stuffed into Halloween costumes. They can't wait to figure out how to shed the obnoxious gear that's been imposed on their bodies.

What if you could have your dog love his new harness, Halloween mask or silly Santa hat? The way he feels about things you drape on his body is going to be directly related to the way you first introduce the new gear to him. You want him to think the things you drape on his body are worth cash and prizes!

Here's a simple formula for introducing new things.

❖ Show him the new thing – "yes" or "click", reward him and then remove the item from view.

❖ Repeat this a few times so the sight of the item predicts that he's going to receive a reward.

❖ Now, present the item and have him touch it or touch it to his body. Again, mark and reward.

❖ Next, touch the new item to the part of the body where it will be going. Repeat, mark and reward a few times.

❖ If it's something you'll be putting over his head, practice rewarding him for remaining still while you take it off and put it on a few times. Before you slip it over his head, lure his snout through it a few times with a delectable yummy and

Kaddi the Street Dog
Kaddi loves costumes because they pay so well!

reward him for sticking his nose through the opening.

- ❖ Put the item on, leave it there for a few seconds, mark and reward, and then remove it

- ❖ Take a break. Put the item out of view for a few minutes. You want the dog to fantasize about you bringing it back out.

- ❖ Put the item back on, leave it on a bit longer. Repeat this step a few more times.

- ❖ Practice walking, coming, sitting, etc. with the item on. Give your dog lots of praise and reinforcement

Continue reinforcing this new "trick," especially in new environments.

Many years ago, my Anja dog taught me about the dangers of putting something on her body without properly taking the time for her to get used to it. Remember, Anja was a feral dog whom I captured in the swamp behind my house. She was close to a year old the first time I took her to Dog Scout Camp. It was time for me to teach the backpacking class. I rushed to the camp store to pick out a beautiful new red backpack for her so I could use her for my demo dog while teaching. Without taking the time to slowly introduce Anja to her new hiking gear, I just dumped it on her back, not even thinking about how scary it might be to her.

Anja and her "dreaded" backpack

For ten years after that, Anja would still lower her head and cower when I'd show her the pack as part of my class demonstration. She was the perfect example of why you need to always introduce new equipment to your dog in a positive, rewarding way. By the way, she'd perk up once the pack was actually on her back as she loved to hike in the woods with it on!

The short time you put into introducing new equipment in a positive way will pay off for both you and your dog in the long run. Have fun!

While you're practicing putting strange clothes on your dog, also spend some time getting him acclimated to wearing a muzzle and being bandaged. In the photo above, Charlie is working on the requirements for his Dog Scout First Aid Badge. He has to get used to being bandaged and wearing a muzzle as part of the requirements for that badge. Kaddi's muzzle is large enough for her to still eat treats while muzzled.

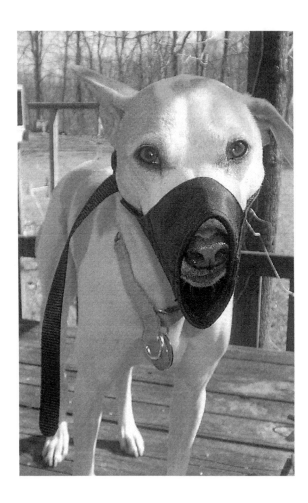

Mystery Solved! 10/17/09

The great peeing mystery may be solved! I called the vet that had done the urinalysis on Charlie the week before he came here, and had them FAX me the lab report. I was surprised that there was chicken scratch looking writing in a few of the columns. I decided to take the paperwork and Charlie with me to the vet appointment I had scheduled later in the day for Reggie. Dr. Mary deciphered the semi-illegible notes to be diagnostic of a UTI (urinary tract infection.) Pretty strange since the clinic up north had told his foster mom that his urine was OK. I ordered him a belly-band yesterday assuming that I might always have a random-peeing dog. Now, I have hope that his peeing issues will be resolved.

Charlie is getting great at his retrieve! I've been tossing all sorts of things for him to pick up, a pop bottle, metal spoon, junk mail and pens. When he doesn't retrieve an object right away, I send one of the other dogs out to pick it up and reward that dog instead. Charlie watches the other dog getting a yummy and usually goes after the object the next time I toss it for him.

He's chasing the Frisbee outside but nowhere near catching it. He loves to chase the udder pull toy and has been doing a bit of wrestle play with Kaddi.

11
PUPPY TRAINING WORKSHEET

Before you get too involved with your new pup, it's a good idea to get the family involved in deciding which vocabulary you want to use with your dog and which family guidelines you're going to have for his behavior. I suggest you sit down with the whole family and jot down some notes. The more *consistent* you are with your pup, the faster he'll learn and the happier you'll be with him.

1. Decide on a vocabulary...

What are the words that family and friends will use consistently with the pup? Here are some examples to get you started:

❖ Come	❖ Stay
❖ Sit	❖ Find it
❖ Down	❖ Go say Hello
❖ Stand	❖ Out
❖ Off	❖ Pick it up
❖ Jump up	❖ Eliminate
❖ Feet up	❖ Jump
❖ Leave it	❖ Go outside
❖ Hold it	❖ Heel
❖ Bring it	❖ Bark
❖ Relax	❖ Go Play
❖ Touch it	❖ Hold still

Which other words do you think you'd like to include in your dog's vocabulary?

2. Which "default" behaviors would you like? Which behaviors would you like the dog to do automatically without being cued? Remember, you've already been working on a default sit when the pup approaches a person who is standing.

* When the pup approaches a sitting person?
* When the pup approaches a reclining person?
* When the pup wants to go out a door?
* When the pup wants a treat?

3. What is the pup already doing that you can put "On Cue?" For example, if your pup is already charging at you, why not add the word "come" as he's approaching

* Coming
* Carrying objects
* Digging
* Barking
* Sitting
* Lying Down

4. Which items is the pup allowed to handle or play with?

* Stuffed animals
* Kid toys
* Sticks
* Balls

5.Which behaviors will you prevent the pup from rehearsing?

* Barking at friends and strangers
* Barking at other dogs
* Grabbing food
* Stealing food
* Guarding food or objects
* Playing "keep away" from humans, with or without objects
* Other...

6. How will the pup learn to be with other dogs, humans and novel places? How will you socialize your pup?

- ❖ Friends, neighbors, other family members
- ❖ Puppy play groups
- ❖ Training classes
- ❖ Dog Clubs
- ❖ Walks
- ❖ Dog friendly businesses
- ❖ Other…

7. What sensitivities does the dog now have?

- ❖ Noises
- ❖ Groups or ages of people
- ❖ Other animals
- ❖ Vehicles
- ❖ Other…

8. What games would you like the dog to learn?

- ❖ Fetch
- ❖ "Find it"
- ❖ Tug and release
- ❖ Frisbee
- ❖ Hide and seek
- ❖ "Go See…"
- ❖ Other…

Again, remember, being _consistent_ is the best gift you can give your pup in helping him learn how best to interact in his world. If you are inconsistent in setting guidelines for your dog, he will be confused about what is rewardable behavior. He's more apt to do behaviors that you find unacceptable. You'll get the impression that he's testing you and trying to drive you crazy when really he's just being himself exploring the world the best he can.

The Dark Side Emerges - 10/21/09

I always tell my clients not to take things personally when their dog does upsetting things. Now, I need to remind myself of my own advice.

Charlie was doing so well. Then I accidently left the gates open. Now he's had a taste of the wild. He vanished when Bob let the dogs out in the evening. Bob was frantic. I found Charlie sitting on the other side of the gate when I drove up the road. Yesterday, I retrieved him from Wendy's house across the street. He was merrily playing with her dogs and seemed oblivious to my calls. Later in the day, as I was checking the fence to make sure it hadn't been knocked down by a fallen tree, he vanished again and was brought home to me by Laura two houses down the road. His freedom to run and play in the fenced yard is suspended for now. He'll either be on a drag line, in the 6' pen or on a cable by the back door when he's outside.

Yet another health problem... I had noticed thin spots of hair on his left cheek that might have been caused by wrestling with the dogs in his foster home. Instead of growing smaller, the patches were becoming more pronounced, so back to the vet we went. Now Charlie has ointment to smear on his demodectic mange patches. At least it's not something that will spread to the other dogs. I'm assuming the lingering UTI has lowered his resistance.

We have lots of training to do to get this little fellow more comfortable with being handled, although he seems friendly enough. He throws little temper tantrums when restrained against his will and definitely is not happy with us when we put the ointment on his face.

He snarled, barked and lunged at two dogs that were in the vet clinic. I'm guessing his time at the pound being the dog they used as the victim for testing dog-aggressive dogs is coming back to haunt us now. He is scared when in the presence of other dogs and restrained on a leash.

12
"MAY I TOUCH YOUR BODY?"

Imagine being a small baby cuddled securely with your Mom. You hear loud jabbering noises and approaching stomping sounds. Within seconds, a squealing giant creature grabs your body and lifts you high away from the security of your warm safe place. You try to wiggle away but the creature holds you ever more tightly. You cry out and wiggle some more. Finally, you give up. There's nothing more you can do. You're too small to fight the monstrous beast that has engulfed you.

Sound like a late night horror movie? Actually, this is the experience shared by many pups early in their lives. The human hands that wanted so much to cuddle and hold them have left an indelible fear-inducing mark on their psyches. As the pups grow, their initial fear reaction is reinforced when the vet techs hold them down for shots or the teens in their new households play rough, grabby games with them with their hands.

At first, the pup seems calm when handled, but as he grows, he appears to get feistier, grabbing at hands and becoming aroused when handled. This can lead to snapping or even biting as he matures. His owners think they're calming him when they attempt to restrain him, but he either shuts down or becomes grabbier; a classic "piranha" puppy.

This problem is so common that many people think it's natural for puppies to be so reactive and bite so much.

To change the puppy so he finds handling rewarding, you will first need to become aware of the signals he's been giving you telling you that he's uncomfortable with approaching human hands.

Begin by slowly moving your hand toward your pup's body. Signs that he's uncomfortable include:

- ❖ Grabbing at your hand as it approaches

- ❖ Backing away from the approaching hand

- ❖ Looking away

❖ Making appeasement signals like licking or collapsing his body

❖ Freezing and showing "whale eye" – the whites of his eyes become more visible

All these signals give you a strong clue that your pup is not as happy with being handled as you may have thought. This is especially common in small dog breeds who've already had lots of experience being cuddled, carried and ogled over by well-meaning admirers.

Identifying Body Sensitivities

This simple exercise will help you to identify areas of your dog's body where he enjoys human touch and those areas that he is less comfortable with human handling and will need to be desensitized.

Make multiple copies of the next page before you start so you will be able to chart your dog's progress over time.

Holding your dog on a leash next to you, gently touch him in each of the marked areas. In the box attached to each arrow, rate your dog's response to being touched in that area. Rate his response as follows:

1. The dog enjoys the touch – he moves toward the hand or has a dreamy look in his eyes as you touch him

2. The dog accepts the touch but tenses slightly – he makes little tongue-flicking appeasement signals or he looks away from you when you touch him

3. The dog gets wiggly and mouthy when you attempt to touch him

4. The dog freezes or gets "whale eye" – his eyes widen so you can see more of the white part of his eye than usual

5. The dog pulls away or tries to escape from the touch

6. The dog cannot be touched in this area – he tries to scoot away or gets extremely wiggly

Date: _____

Family Member/
Friend:_____

Have everyone in the family fill out one of these charts. Your dog will respond differently to each person. Date and label each chart with the family member's name.

The *May I Touch Your Body?"* Game

This game will reward your dog for being touched. You'll need some very high quality small treats and a quiet place away from distractions. Have your dog on a leash attached to the front ring of his harness so he'll be able to sit facing you while you sit on the floor near him.

- ❖ Gently reach toward your dog with your hand relaxed but with an open palm.

- ❖ As you say "May I touch your side," gently press the ends of your fingers against the side of your dog.

- ❖ Wait until he relaxes under your touch, say "Yes" and give him a treat.

- ❖ Repeat touching his side, marking his calm, relaxed behavior with a "yes," and then rewarding him

- ❖ After a few trials of this sequence move on to other body parts; "May I touch your chest, head, toes, etc."

- ❖ Play this game a few times daily. Be patient. Take it as slowly as you need to so that your dog becomes relaxed being touched all over his body.

- ❖ Once he's comfortable being handled by you, it's time to teach this game to your friends so your dog will learn to generalize the game with other people.

So how do you change your pup's impression of being handled?

- ❖ Stop all family members and friends from playing grabbing games with your pup. Forget the well-meaning wrestling. Your little guy has no idea that this is really supposed to be fun. It's intimidating bullying and has to stop immediately.

- ❖ Work through the body sensitivity chart with each family member. This will give you a baseline idea of how sensitive your pup is to being touched.

- ❖ Play the *May I Touch Your Body?* game with your pup.

- ❖ Teach your pup to hand target. This will make approaching a hand a rewardable trick. (See *Hand Targeting,* Chapter 9)

- ❖ Resist letting all your friends grab and cuddle your pup. Teach them the body touching game and make their touching rewardable for your dog. Teach them to play the eye contact game with the pup and he'll get great at sitting and smiling at newcomers.

- ❖ Teach your pup the *Sit to be Petted Game* as described later in this book.

Buzz has learned to enjoy being cuddled and is much less grabby with kids since he's been playing the *May I Touch Your Body?* game

Do you wonder what will happen if you don't make an effort to change your pup's opinion of human hands? You've probably already met dogs who get excited and jumpy when they meet new people or maybe you've met the ones who snap at kids when they try to pet the dog. You don't want your dog to be nervous every time a hand moves in his direction. Do your homework ahead of time and you'll help your pup become the relaxed confident guy you'll be proud to introduce to others.

"Chin"

Now that your pup is not flinching as your hand approaches, you're ready to move on to one of my favorite dog behaviors: your dog will learn to rest his chin gently on your hand. We call this trick "chin."

Once he knows this trick, you'll think of many uses for it:

- ❖ Calming your dog while he's sitting or standing next to you

- ❖ Holding your dog's face for vet exams

- ❖ Pointing his head away from distractions (I often gently move Kaddi's head away from staring at other dogs.)

- ❖ You can expand the trick to teach him to rest his chin on the floor or other objects of your choosing. This makes for very cute pictures!

You'll start by slowly moving your open hand toward your dog, palm up, and gently touching your dog's chin. "Click" and give him a reward.

This sounds so simple, but many dogs will move their heads away. Your dog may not be as comfortable with your touch as you assume him to be. Be patient, you may have to shape this trick a tiny bit at a time.

Blaze and his mom Josephine practice the *Chin* game. Blaze was very uncomfortable having his head and face touched and would often grab at people's hands.

Work to increase your dog's acceptance of the chin touch, little by little, "clicking" each time he accepts more of your hand under his chin. Your goal will be to have him resting his chin in your cupped hand. Practice doing this trick and then add the cue word "chin" as a signal to do the behavior.

Lacey practices chin targeting on a chair.

Blaze

"I adopted a $1\frac{1}{2}$ year old rescue dog, a border collie-husky mix. We are his fourth residence in his short 18 months of life. We renamed him "Blaze." Blaze and I were greatly in need of training, and I had the good fortune to find Beth within the first two weeks of Blaze joining our family.

I have always had dogs in my life and had been through traditional dog obedience training with all of them. My last experience with dog obedience training, though, had been 13 years ago and the idea of positive dog training was completely new to me.

Through the various exercises Beth taught us, Blaze is able to learn to make the right choices. I can see the gears turning when he is sitting there figuring out what behavior will get him his positive reward. When he performs the desired action, that behavior is immediately marked so that he knows for certain what got him the praise and reward and what it is he is supposed to do. Beth taught us many exercises (games to Blaze): Eye Contact Game, Bad Dog Retrieve, Go Find, Crate Game, Walk Away Game, Go to Mat. One that had an immediate and dramatic result is called "Chin." Blaze absolutely did not like to be touched anywhere around his mouth. His whiskers would tighten and he would nip, not as though to bite, but as though to say 'please don't touch me there.' He needs to be comfortable with being touched around his mouth, though, as eventually that gentle nip could advance to something more serious, and for various reasons, such as a vet exam, or if we need him to relinquish something harmful out of his mouth. Within 30 minutes of being taught this exercise, we were able to say "Chin" and Blaze would stop nipping and lay his chin in the palms of our hands."

Josephine Busch

Getting Ready for Vet Visits

Your vet will love you and your pup if you take the time to practice the *May I Touch Your Body* and *Chin* games. Pups often become overwhelmed when the vet tech restrains them for simple exams or offers to clip the pup's toenails.

You can prepare your pup ahead of time for the handling he may receive during a vet exam.

- ❖ Have friends play the *May I Touch Your Body?* game with your pup. Make sure you include both males and females, young and old.

- ❖ Practice touching his toenails. Reward him for being near the sound of the toenail clippers. Gradually get him used to having the tips of his toenails clipped.

- ❖ Practice a "vet hold" on your dog: restrain him by wrapping one arm around his chest and the other arm over his back and holding up his chin. (see photo below)

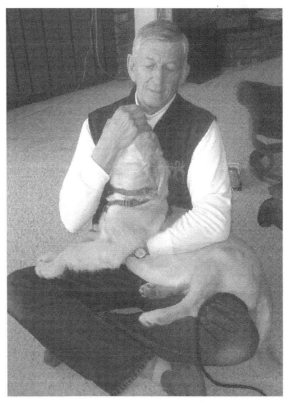

- ❖ Teach your dog *The Mat Game* (Chapter 27), and then take your mat with you when you visit the vet. Make sure you put the mat under your dog on the cold steel examination table and he'll be much more relaxed.

- ❖ Stop in and visit your vet at times other than your scheduled appointments. Bring lots of treats and have your pup practice his tricks there.

Make sure you stick up for the safety of your pup. Some vets still think it's OK to forcibly hold a pup down to examine him. That can cause him to become more frightened of the vet clinic over time. Instead, have your pup used to being handled before he goes in for his vet visits so he'll be comfortable being examined. Both your pup and your vet will be grateful!

Dick is practicing holding Darse so she'll think it's a fun game when she's restrained during a vet visit.

Escapee– 10/26/09

After last week's escapes, I had to step back and look at Charlie's needs and my training methods. I realized that the "escaping dog" problem was triggering my own old reactive ideas about training. I was thinking about how I could "stop" the behavior rather than how I could insert a more desirable behavior instead.

First of all, the slipping away behavior started when I became lax about accompanying Charlie outside. He's a smart little guy who bores easily so I need to keep him engaged rather than letting him plan his own fun activities. I'm also musing about turning fence jumping into a rewardable trick like stealing when I teach the *Bad Dog Retrieve.*

Charlie jumped the fence once and I immediately followed him over. After slight hesitation (He got that sneaky eyed "I think I'm going to run away" look) he bounded back to me and I rewarded him heavily. I need to devise some calling across the fence games and calling in the road in front of the house games. I'm also working on the neighbors' barking dogs as a cue to come to me for a reward. This seems to be working very well.

I also need to be a better manager. Charlie will be on a line outside when it's dark out and I can't see him to do a recall. We'll use the cable tie out for short pee breaks in the dark.

We started work on "go to your mat" today. Charlie hasn't figured out what to do yet. He's experimenting with behaviors much less than I expected. It's going to take some work to get his brain used to trying new things out near people.

I signed up for a beginners training class with my old friend Sharon. I think Charlie and I will have a great time!

13
SOCIALIZATION VS. SENSITIZATION

Imagine you are traveling to a strange country with customs you don't know, meeting people who dress funny, gesticulate in strange ways and say things you wish you could translate. Their driving habits are beyond horrendous and you've only been scared out of your wits six times in the last five minutes.

Now, think of what it must be like for your new dog going to town with you.

We've all read the dog books that tell us we should take our dogs to thousands of places and meet thousands of people so they'll be socialized. I've refined my thinking on that. I think it's most important for a dog to feel safe and secure with his family and at his own home before shoving him into the world of barking dogs, screaming kids and honking trucks. Chris Bach calls this "developing a safety history" with our dogs.

There are plenty of reasons to carefully consider where and when you're going to take your new dog to learn about the world.

Remember those holiday festivities of your childhood when some auntie you only saw once a year gave you a slimy bad breath kiss and a big hug. Did you wish you could punch her in the gut and tell her to get out of your space? You didn't though, because you were a little kid and she was a big grown-up. Think of what it must be like for a puppy to be handed off and hugged and ogled over by noisy strangers. He might wish he could bite them but is too overwhelmed to show his fear. Often dogs that are allowed to be grabbed and smooched by strangers as pups become snappy and grumpy when meeting new people as they grow into maturity and are a bit braver about protecting themselves.

First of all, your dog needs to be comfortable with *your* touch and handling before you branch out and let others pet and handle him. Work through the *Body Sensitivity Chart* (in this chapter) and then practice the *May I Touch Your Body?* (Chapter 12) game. Your dog needs to be confident and calm when you handle him before you can expect him to tolerate being handled by strangers.

Once your pup feels safe with your handling, selectively introduce him to others. That means don't just hand the little guy off to anyone who thinks he looks cute. Help children pet him gently using slow relaxing strokes. Especially be alert for those who think petting a dog means playing those intimidating grabbing, face wrestling or arousing tousling and teasing games. One of the best ways to get your pup to be comfortable with other people is to have other people practice the *Don't Eat the Hand that Feeds You*, *Eye Contact*, (Chapter 5) and *May I Touch Your Body?* games with your dog. Your dog will learn to calm himself and be an Einstein in the presence of new people while the people are being kept busy interacting with your dog in ways that keep *them* from scaring him by doing obnoxious petting or otherwise roughing him up and triggering a "lizard brain" response.

When you are thinking of taking your pup to new environments, you need to consider a number of factors:

❖ Will you have time to pay attention to your dog's behavior and train him where you are taking him? Remember, your dog is always learning whether you're part of the process or not. That means he could be learning to jump on people or grab food from little kids' hands if you take him to a group event and you're not constantly aware of what he's doing.

❖ Is the place or event a calm enough setting where your dog will be able to function enough to take treats and be rewarded for behaviors you like. Some people get a bit confused about what it means to "socialize" their dog. They think that means taking your dog everywhere with you no matter how potentially scary the event could be to him.

Beware: If you take your puppy somewhere and he seems to act like an angel - not the frolicking busy puppy you know at home - he may be just "*shut-down*," not actually well-behaved. The quiet behavior you are seeing is a fear reaction. Get your puppy out of that environment as fast as you can. Fears he acquires as a pup can stick with him through his entire life.

I learned my lesson about the difference between socialization and sensitization many years ago. We had only had our new Belgian Sheepdog puppy a couple of weeks when our town held its annual hot air balloon festival. I remember spending a couple of hours lazing on a lawn chair in my backyard watching dozens of brightly colored giant balloons float over our house. My new pup, Jacques, was about 12 weeks old. He normally was a very busy guy, but he was cuddly while the balloons flew over our house. I remember him lying with me on my chest as we watched the beautiful spectacle passing over our heads.

We thought our puppy Jacques was being cuddly when he spent the afternoon lying on my lap as we watched the hot-air balloons pass overhead. He was really terrified and shut down. For the rest of his life he panicked anytime he saw or heard a balloon in the neighborhood.

My mistake was thinking that Jacques was enjoying the show. He was actually scared and completely shut down. The next year, when a few balloons appeared in the sky over our house, Jacques panicked and took off running. We found him staggering up the road four hours later. He was near heat stoke and his feet were so worn from running that his pads were bloody. For the rest of Jacques' life, we had "hot air balloon alerts." We'd watch and listen for balloons so we could hide poor Jacques safely in the house with the doors and windows closed as they flew by.

I also erred in taking my Kaddi puppy out to scary places more than I should have. She's now a wonderful traveler who can work in schools and giant convention centers where I do my wolf education and dog training educational programs. She's a completely different dog when I enter the parking lot of the local pet store. She flattens herself on the car seat and quivers. She still remembers how scary this place was ten years ago, when I took her there as a pup.

Remember, your job is to keep your pup safe. Your pup is relying on you to help him explore the world.

A word about dog parks...

We all fantasize about our dogs running, playing and having a great time. Some of us are lucky to have large yards where our dogs can exercise but many people have no place for their dogs to be off leash and burn off their doggy energy. Dog parks have become the "fantasy" place for our dogs to socialize and use their exuberant energy

The problem is that the fantasy of going to a dog park can easily turn into a nightmare for you and your dog. Not only can your dog learn "tricks" you never wanted him to learn, he could be injured or forever sensitized to other dogs.

One day, my training client and I took her three gorgeous Rhodesian Ridgebacks to a new dog park in our community. No one else was there and we had a wonderful time watching her dogs stretch their legs and float effortlessly over the acreage.

As we were preparing to leave, a couple of women arrived at the park with three mixed breed dogs of varying sizes. We called over the fence to them and asked them to give us a couple of minutes to get Judy's dogs leashed and out of the enclosure before they entered. We had no idea how Judy's dogs would act if a new family of dogs came in. It was easier to leave and skip the doggie introductions. The women voiced their frustration that we were leaving, "How are our dogs ever going to play with other dogs if you leave? Aren't dog parks where dogs are supposed to meet new friends?"

As we passed by the women on the way out, I heard one of the women say to her friend, "How is my dog ever going to get over his _dog aggression_ if no one will let their dogs play with him?"

You see, you may know that your dog is great with other dogs, you just have no idea of the bite history of the other dogs entering the park! What if that big dog charging toward yours has a history of bullying other dogs?

I haven't spent much time in dog parks nor do I plan to. I've never had any of my dogs in one. The times I entered as a sightseer, I saw numerous examples of dogs bullying each other. I saw dogs who had to defend themselves by getting snarly or running to their moms to hide. I saw very scary situations where dogs were chasing other dogs in a predatory manner. This is all a recipe for disaster. At Dog Scout Camp in Michigan, we have a wonderful fenced dog play area. Our goal is to have dogs safely play with each other without becoming reactive. We have a sign on the door to keep people from entering randomly, "Please wait" or "It's OK to enter." When someone new wants to come in, all of us call and leash our dogs so we can release them one at a time to greet the new dog. We watch our dogs' play closely, making sure no "play" involves ganging up on another dog. We use our time to practice our training. We practice calling our dogs away from play. This is a stark contrast to the dog parks I visited, where I saw people casually sitting at picnic tables or chatting on their cell phones, hardly watching their dogs at all.

Remember, socializing your dog means gradually introducing him to people, places and other dogs so he can become more comfortable with his world. Be careful to protect him from situations that could scar him for life, physically or emotionally.

Happy dogs in the play yard at Dog Scout Camp

Sensitivity Assessment Chart

This chart is going to help you assess the various sensitivities of your dog. Perhaps your dog is somewhat scared during thunderstorms, or maybe he gets a bit nervous around screaming little kids. You will rate each of these sensitivities on a scale of 0 – 10, **zero** meaning that the dog isn't the least bit fazed by the stimulus, and **10,** meaning the dog is pretty scared, upset, or agitated by that particular stimulus. The chart lists some of the more common things dogs might get upset about, but there are blanks for you to fill in any others you can think of. For example, if your dog never even notices thunderstorms, but gets a little nervous around men and has been known to freak out at people wearing hats, you would fill in **nothing** on the thunderstorm column but perhaps rate him at **3** for the "men" column and **10** for the "People wearing hats" column.

Think about any special fears your dog might have. Maybe a kid almost ran over him with a bike once. He still quivers a little when bicycles go by. You would add that item in one of the spare columns.

Your job is to be aware of these sensitivities and work to systematically lower as many as possible. For example, if your dog has a thing about people in hats, start by having friends with whom he is otherwise comfortable, wear hats. Make each experience with a "hat person" as positive as possible through having the person treat or play favorite games with the dog. Then gradually help him to have good experiences with others wearing hats.

Protect your dog from situations that are more than he can handle. Work slowly. Be patient. Don't force the dog into situations that he cannot handle. He will progress best if <u>he</u> consciously chooses to deal with somewhat frightening people or other stimuli. Avoid coaxing, bribing, and luring.

There is a difference between fears that are based on his inexperience and fears that come from events that were traumatic to him. He may never overcome fears that are based on bad events in his life. Although you may seem to make some progress in desensitizing him to these fears, they may resurface. Never assume that the dog is now "cured" of his former fears.

Make multiple copies of the sensitivity chart and keep track of your pup's progress over time. Good luck!

Sensitivity Assessment Chart

Date _____

	Loud Noises	Human Hands	Other Dogs	Strangers	Vacuum Sweeper									
10														
9														
8														
7														
6														
5														
4														
3														
2														
1														

Level	Loud Noises	Human Hands	Other Dogs	Strangers	Vacuum Sweeper	Garbage Trucks	Running Kids
10							
9	■						
8	■	■				■	
7	■	■		■		■	
6	■	■		■		■	
5	■	■		■		■	
4	■	■	■	■		■	
3	■	■	■	■		■	
2	■	■	■	■		■	■
1	■	■	■	■		■	■

In this example, we could imagine a dog named Princess who is fearful of loud noises, doesn't like to be petted all that much, is leery of strange people and hates garbage trucks. Can you see how she'd be over the top if a garbage truck was going by just as a stranger was petting her? There is an additive effect when the two fearful things are experienced at the same time. The owners might be surprised when their dear pet snapped at or bit the person who was petting her. She hadn't ever done that before, but having the two scary things happen at the same time has pushed her beyond her limits of tolerance.

Author Nicole Wilde has a nice book for dealing with your dog's fear issues: *Help for your Fearful Dog*: http://phantompub.com/

Your job is to work to get your dog more comfortable with all the things that might be frightening or arousing to him. Work on one sensitivity at a time and keep records of your progress.

Socialization Diary

You may want to use a "Socialization Diary" to help you keep track of your progress in introducing new people and experiences to your pup. Here's an example that might show how our friend Princess is progressing:

Date	Experience	Pup's Reaction	Comments
5/20/2010	Took Princess for a walk up the block	Princess liked meeting the neighbors but wanted to jump all over them.	I forgot to take treats with me. I could have had my neighbors practice a lured "sit" with her. I'll remember next time.
5/25/2010	Vet appointment	Princess liked meeting everyone and never even noticed getting her shot.	I'm glad I got her used to being touched. She did the "chin" trick for the vet tech. I had special yummy treats for her.
5/30/2010	Took Princess to pick up the kids at a soccer game	Princess was very wiggly and grabby with the kids	This was too much for my pup. I think the screaming kids scared her. Next time I'll invite a few quiet kids to practice the "sit" game with her
6/10/2010	Princess went with us to the farmers' market	She pulled a lot on the leash and started barking like crazy at the other dogs there	Yet another miscalculation on my part. Our poor pup was scared and unable to concentrate and respond to our cues
6/17/2010	Back to the farmers market but we sat off to the side away from the crowds	Princess had a great time showing off her tricks to some friendly people who were admiring her	I think Princess had a much better time. She never barked. When we saw other dogs in the distance, we gave her lots of treats for looking at us too.
6/22/2010	Another vet trip – just for fun	I stopped in the vet clinic and asked if I could take Princess into an exam room they weren't using. We practiced our tricks there	Princess was so cute and so happy!! She loves everyone at the vet clinic.
7/4/2010	Fourth of July Holiday	We played in the basement this evening and Princess had lots of treats	I'm glad my vet warned me to be careful and not let Princess get scared of the sounds of my neighbors setting off fireworks! We were careful to potty her before dark and keep her in a quiet place during the noisy evening.

7/5/2010	Family Picnic	We had a gang of people here. Princess scared little Jenny when she jumped on her and grabbed her stuffed animal,	I screwed up. I should have been watching what was going on. Maybe I should have spent time teaching the little kids how to do tricks with Princess instead of terrorizing them.
7/10/2010	Playing with the neighbor's dog	Princess got to play with Toby, a very gentle Golden who lives two houses down from us.	Princess & Toby were great together! We didn't let my neighbor's other dog out to play – he's old & grouchy and I didn't want Princess to have a bad experience
7/15/2010	Scary garbage trucks	I saved some left over roast from last evening's dinner and had Princess do tricks while the garbage trucks were driving by.	Princess looked scared for just a second, but then decided doing tricks was more fun. Boy, does she like roast beef! I'll do the same next week.

Socialization Diary

Date	Experience	Pup's Reaction	Comments

Watch-Out for Scary Monsters!

Do you remember the wicked witch in the fairy tail who wanted to lure Hansel and Gretel into her little cottage so she could bake them into cookies? Picture her, bent over, hand outstretched, coaxing the kids to come to her.

If your dog is scared of some people, the last thing you want is for them to try to coax your dog up to them. Your pup will just become more scared. He may lunge forward to get a treat but then will bounce away as fast as he can.

Do not let people attempt to coax your scared dog! Here are some other alternatives:

- ❖ It's easiest to just keep your dog away from scary people but, you really do need to get him used to all categories of humans eventually, so you'll need to work on his fears a bit at a time. If your dog is petrified of teens wearing backpacks, get him used to you wearing a backpack first. If people wearing hats send him into a frenzy, desensitize him to hats by having his favorite family members wear them.

- ❖ Have scary people avoid staring, leaning toward, or sticking their arms out toward your dog. Give them something different to do; perhaps ask them to look off to the side and turn sideways.

- ❖ Have the person your dog is scared of toss treats behind the dog. You're not trying to lure the dog to the person, but rather telling the dog he can leave the scary person, if he wants to. Often this method changes the dog's idea about the person being scary and the dog will start approaching on his own.

- ❖ If the dog is brave enough to approach, have the stranger feed the dog a tidbit and then take a step back. Repeat this a few times and often the dog will relax and willingly approach the person.

Many people are overbearing with dogs they do not know. They'll want to grab, cuddle, or pick-up your dog. You wouldn't hand over your human kid to be hugged by a stranger. Likewise, you need to be protective of your "dog kid." Your dog should not have to be petted by everyone. It's OK to say, "No, my dog doesn't feel like being petted right now."

What works best is giving new acquaintances other tasks to do with your dog. Let them hold a treat and play the *Eye Contact Game* or the *Don't Eat the Hand Game* (Chapter 5). Your dog may learn to anticipate meeting new people and his fear will be a thing of the past. If, however, he doesn't always want to meet new people, it's your responsibility keep him feeling safe. Not everyone needs to pet your dog.

More Help for Fearful Dogs

When Kaddi was a puppy, we discovered that she was much less fearful and reactive when she was wearing clothes. We'd never even owned a dog coat for any of our previous dogs, but since Kaddi was from Africa and had an extremely short coat, we had pity on her and started collecting a winter wardrobe for her.

We began to notice that some clothes seemed to help her be less fearful than others. We suspected that the tighter fitting outfits worked much like swaddling an infant; she felt more secure when she was tightly bundled up.

A few years ago, a new pet product was introduced that seems to have the same affect. "Thundershirts™" have helped many fearful dogs reduce their level of anxiety. They're worth a try (and fully guaranteed) if your dog is dealing with fear issues.

Kaddi modeling her Thundershirt™
Too bad Kaddi didn't invent these or she'd be a rich dog today!

To order Thundershirts, go to: www.thundershirt.com

Tellington Touch is special body work that can help your dog with both physical and psychological challenges. We've used it with all of our fearful dogs. You should be able to find a trained practitioner in your area.

Get more information about *Tellington Touch* at: www.ttouch.com

Reggie came to us with back problems. His friend Heather Ross is a Tellington Touch practitioner who visits with him regularly.

You may also want to experiment with using D.A.P., Dog Appeasing Pheromone. This product is available as a spray, scented collar or a room atomizer. It often helps reduce fear and stress-related behavior in dogs. You can find D.A.P products at your local pet store.

Be patient and caring of your sensitive dog. Protect him from scary things and nurture his confidence. With patience and empathy, he will improve over time.

Kaddi was very fearful as a young dog. She barked, growled or shook in the presence of people she didn't know, especially kids. We never reprimanded her. We used the *Sensitivity Chart* to help chart her progress over time and worked to help her overcome her fears using positive training methods. She is now a sweet, grounded friend to all the kids she meets.

Tricks - 10-30-09

Charlie has been here 3 ½ weeks and will soon be our little guy forever. In the last few days, he's coming more alive – both for good and bad.

His escaping from the yard was upsetting me. I really don't want a dog that I can't ever trust loose to run and play so we decided to add two feet of fencing to the side of the yard where he's been pulling his vanishing acts. I let Charlie come out and inspect my handiwork while I was putting the finishing touches on the project. While I stood watching, he flattened himself on his side and started scooting *under* the fence. After all this fence heightening, he may have been going under instead of over all along! I piled branches along the fence to thwart his efforts. Who knows what his next trick will be.

Charlie is really starting to catch on to all this trick stuff. I spent a couple of short training sessions working on the *Go to Your Mat* trick. He's now doing it like a pro. I can send him out about 6 feet to his mat and am now starting to work on having him sit on the mat when he gets there.

Today we did a big school program for about 200 kids. He ran around the auditorium greeting the kids. It's so nice having a dog that's less fearful. I can see it's also going to be a problem keeping this little guy from totally losing track of me in his enthusiasm!

He did gorgeous retrieves, went to his mat, and even jumped the little agility jump with his dumbbell in his mouth. I was amazed as were the kids and teachers.

He automatically runs to his crate to be fed so now I'm working on calling him from the crate when he charges in and then having him sit, down or heel before I send him back to the crate.

14
YOUR DOG'S NAME, THE PROMISE OF RICHES TO COME!

"Hey, Spot, get over here!!"

"Stop that, Spot!"!

"Spot, you stupid dog, you're peeing all over the floor!"

"Good Spot, Good Spot"

"Spot! Drop that shoe!"

Ok, so if you were Spot the dog, what kind of associations would you have with your name? Would it have any meaning to you at all or would it mean that the big scary human monster was going to be chasing you down and grabbing you? Think of your poor pup. Do you want him to be scared when he hears his name or do you want him to come running joyfully to you?

Training your pup to respond to his name takes some purposeful action on your part. You want him to associate his name with good things happening in his life, not predicting that you're chasing him, ripping his favorite "chew trophies" from his mouth, or screaming in his face.

You can easily teach your dog to love hearing his name and become attentive to you.

First of all, if you are adopting a dog who already has a name, consider renaming him. If his former family has used his name to yell at him or if they've used his name without giving it meaning to the dog, his name may already have become a "poisoned cue" to him. It may be a verbal signal that is either ignored or causes your pup to become anxious. When we got Charlie Darwin, his name was "Woodie." Since his previous owners dumped him at a kill shelter because he was causing so much trouble in their lives, I'm guessing that his name meant, "run away fast in the other direction," to him. At least, he showed no sign of coming to his name when we got him.

To train your new dog, get some great treats and introduce him to his new name by saying his name and immediately giving him a treat. Repeat this a few times. Now say his name in every tone of voice you might ever use to call him and reward him each time.

Wait a few minutes; don't say anything to your dog. Repeat saying the name and rewarding him. By now, he should be hoping very hard that you'll say his name. He is making very positive associations with his name. His name is now worth cash and prizes!

Practice this game a few times each day until you can see your dog buddy perk up and look happy when he hears his name.

Be aware of how often and in what circumstances you're tempted to use his name. The hard task for you is to **not** poison this cue. You don't want to have him associate his name with you chasing him, grabbing him, or yelling at him, or to not even notice his name because you're saying it so much. If you're strung out and peeved at your pet, take a deep breath and remember: you want your pet to be responsive to you and not scared of you. The sound of his name should fill your dog with happy anticipation.

More Management - 11/3/09

I'm realizing what a fragmented trainer I am. I just updated my training chart and was hit with the realization that I wasn't being all that organized about my training routine. My schedule has been more than hectic and I've been doing my training in the cracks in between. The good news is that Charlie is learning so much anyway! Maybe that's why doing this journal is so important. With lots of management and consistency he's already doing so well.

Most important, he's learning that Bob and I are worth being with and interacting with. That's what it's all about – forming a relationship with this little guy so we can be buddies.

Charlie is becoming a relaxed member of our family and learning lots of new stuff. Last evening, we practiced our first "empty beer can retrieve." Charlie will be going with me next week to do wolf education in Upper Michigan hunting camps. His new skill will serve him well as he noses around the hunting camps embarrassing sloppy hunters by finding their empty beer cans tossed in the leaf litter of the woods.

I'm also seeing the rough edges I need to work on. Later today, I may plant myself in the corner of the vet clinic and work on rewarding Charlie for non-reactive behavior.

We've been preventing problems by doing lots of management.

❖ Charlie is never loose outside unless we're out there to watch him. Bob bought these very strange little flashlight-glow stick things. We've been attaching one to Charlie's harness when we send him out in the dark. We love watching this blue glowing wand bounce around our yard.

❖ If we're in the yard and too busy to keep track of him, he's safely tethered (actually chained on a light-weight chain– he knows how to slice through a long line with a couple of chews) This might sound evil, but it's actually a nice way he can get used to lying quietly near us while we are working in the yard. This is a lot better in the long run than letting him cruise the yard looking for escape routes.

❖ Charlie is never loose in the house unless we're available to keep track of him. This morning, he got the cute idea of running off with my sock just as I was getting ready to jump into the shower. Back into his crate he went. We're not going to play the "steal stuff" game.

❖ We're using a bit of "negative punishment". That means decreasing the frequency of a behavior we don't like by removing something he likes. Actually, it's also just plain management but timed so it can be a learning experience. I am using the marker "bummer" when he has earned the chance to go back to his crate for behavior I consider obnoxious.

- ❖ He can hang out on our bed with us as long as he isn't attempting to eat our hands or bedding. If his behavior becomes obnoxious, he's back into his crate until we have more time to interact with him in a positive way. We may let him back out a few minutes later for a second try. The effectiveness of this training is seen when he comes back onto the bed and stretches out, relaxed, without the obnoxious behavior.

- ❖ I also put him into his crate when he attempts to engage our dogs by barking in their faces. This behavior has become rare since I've been consistent about removing him from the scene immediately when it starts.

- ❖ Barking when the neighborhood dogs bark - I removed Charlie from the scene and stuffed him in the house when he started recreational barking answering the dogs across the street. I don't want him to develop the habit of barking just because he hears a bark in the distance

- ❖ He's rewarded with petting and attention when he's calm on the bed.

- ❖ He's rewarded for bringing anything to us.

- ❖ He's rewarded for sitting when he wants our attention.

Wild Charlie on the run! Notice that he's still wearing a drag line.

A Word on "No Reward Markers" and Putting Your Dog Away in his Crate

There's a lot of discussion among dog trainers about whether it's ever appropriate to teach your dog a word that lets him know that his current behavior is not rewardable. It's very easy for dog owners to become addicted to yelling at their dogs. Their making "ach" or "no" commands can serve to temporarily suppress or interrupt their dog's behavior, but they're not really teaching the dog a behavior to replace the behavior they don't like.

I tell my clients that putting their dog away in his crate when he's driving them crazy is a way to maintain a good relationship with their dog. It's a lot better to put the dog somewhere safely away from you than to scream at or otherwise scare your dog to suppress his behavior. Of course, you aren't putting your dog in his crate to punish him. Hopefully, you've spent time teaching him that his crate is a cool place to hang out. (see *Crates, Confinement, Poops & Human Sanity*, Chapter 21)

Many dogs seem to be like little human toddlers when they're over-tired. Just like the two year-old child who throws temper tantrums or runs wildly around the house shortly before bedtime, puppies often will get a case of the "super zoomies" when they're exhausted. They become hyperactive, grab hands and act crazed. That's a good time to safely put your pup in his crate.

In Charlie's case, I added the word "bummer" to mark the less desirable behavior. I don't think he was suffering from the zoomies. He had just learned that eating people on the bed was fun. The "bummer" word was informational not a suppressor. "You eat human hands and you get to go to your crate!" – simple cause and effect. For Charlie, his crate is not a bad place, he associates it with eating and curling up for a nice nap. The effect of this "negative punishment" (taking away something that he liked) decreased his obnoxious behavior very quickly. If he wanted to schmooze on our bed, he had to be as unobtrusive as possible.

Kiah

"One of the most important things we learned while training with Beth was the Hand targeting and *May I Touch Your Body*. Our Siberian hated to be touched but learned quickly if she let us touch her she was rewarded. Of course. learning tricks is always fun and Kiah has learned to amuse herself in the summer taking things in and out of the swimming pool. Our Husky has grown into a well balanced dog with gentle training. This is the best way to train.

Thanks for all of your help,"

Chris & Steve Whitney

15
"COME!"

I'm amazed at how many people I meet who are mad because their dog doesn't "obey" them and come when they call. They think that their dog is somehow blowing them off. They take it personally and get angry. Their dog should know what to do!

That's pretty crazy when you think about it. Could you learn math or physics by someone screaming at you? You learn best incrementally, increasing your skills with time and practice.

You need to think of training your dog to come as a skill that is nurtured with time and practice. Your dog will learn the basic skill and then improve with practice and positive reinforcement.

Your first task is to manage your pup so he never learns to play the "na-na-na-na na, you can't catch me game." That means your pup should be on a leash or drag line so you can help him get the answer right. You never want to call him and not be able to help him come. That's one of the best ways to poison your "come" cue.

You'll begin training "come" the same way you taught him his name. Say "come" and immediately give him a very high value treat. Repeat this in every tone of voice you can think of. Wait a few minutes and repeat the process. Now, step back a foot or two and repeat. Your pup most likely will move toward you. Reward him with the scrumptious treat.

Step back again. Say your pup's name and "come" in a cheery voice. When the pup moves to you, say "yes" and reward him. Practice this increasing the distance, or going out of sight around corners.

Never just stand there helplessly watching your dog not move or move away from you. We don't want the cue "come" to become meaningless "jabber" from your mouth. Do something to help the pup get the answer right. If he loses focus in coming in your direction, you can step on the cord to prevent him from scooting away and either gently encourage him to come toward you by reeling in the cord or walk up to him and give him the food. (I know this sounds dumb since he didn't move but it's better than just standing there doing nothing.)

Practice this new trick at varying distances, in different locations, always with a leash or drag line on the pup so he never has a chance to make a mistake.

Now, if you think your dog is going to magically come charging to you in all situations once you've done this training, forget it. This is just the beginning of your recall training. Your job will be to teach this new trick to perfection with lots of distances and with many distractions. **Don't expect your pup to magically obey you if you haven't done your training homework**. Just remember, the time you spend purposefully training this trick will be a gift that allows your pup more interesting choices of things to do with you in the future. Stick with it.

Advanced Come – Restrained Recalls & Hide & Seek

Would you like to have your dog absolutely LOVE to come to you? These games will help you perfect your recall so your dog will come to you lightning fast even when he can't see where you are.

You'll need an assistant. If you can get the whole family to help, the games will be even more fun.

You'll want to have a harness on your dog and either a drag line, if you're playing inside, or a long line if you are playing outside. The line needs to be attached to the back ring of the harness so there's no pressure on the dog's neck.

- ❖ One person holds the dog. The other person waves a great treat under the dog's nose and moves away quickly. The dog will most likely strain a bit on the line.

- ❖ The person who moved away calls the dog.

- ❖ The restraining person holds the dog just a second longer than the dog wants and then releases the dog to run to the other person.

- ❖ As the dog approaches, the caller steps on the line and lures the dog into a sit.

Round Robin Recall

For this variation of the *Come* game you'll simply spread your family and friends out into a big circle.

- ❖ One person holds the pup's line while someone else across the circle calls the dog

- ❖ As the dog approaches the caller, she'll step on the line and have the dog sit and reward the dog

- ❖ Then someone else in the circle calls the dog and the process is repeated

Hide and seek

Dogs love this game! You're going to add a new cue for this game. Your dog is going to begin practicing to stay in one place as you walk away, even out of sight. You'll have to decide what cue you choose to use, either "wait" or "stay."

- ❖ One person holds the dog on a long line attached to the back ring of the dog's harness.

- ❖ The second person tells the dog to "stay," and takes off at a fast pace. (You can have the dog sit first, if you like.) The dog is staying by default because he's being held by the first handler. It's OK. He'll start to learn the cue. The quick movement of the person who is moving away will keep the dog's attention on that person, who will be calling him.

- ❖ The second person calls the dog with animation. You want the dog to be excited about this game!

At first, Charlie had no response to being called. Now, after lots of practice and rewards, he turns on a dime and charges to us.

- ❖ As the dog comes charging to him, the caller steps on the long line and then has the dog do a nice sit.

- ❖ Repeat this sequence and call the dog over longer distances.

- ❖ As the dog catches on to this fun game, start challenging his tracking and finding skills by having the caller hide behind the house, bushes, trees, or whatever else is available.

Caution: Make sure the sender doesn't have the long line tangled around her legs before she sends the dog or this could become a dangerous game.

Also, when stepping on the long line to prevent the dog from bouncing away after coming, make sure you always slow the dog gently rather than having him come to an abrupt stop as he hits the end of the line. Let a bit of the line slide under your foot as you gradually increase foot pressure on the line. You'll be putting the "brakes on" gradually rather than jerking the dog to a stop.

Dogs can learn to be evasive when they're having a good time running in the yard. Remember the "na, na, na, na, na, you can't catch me game?" Now that your dog is charging toward you when you call, and has practiced sitting as he comes to you, start grabbing and holding his collar each time he comes. That way, if you really need to grab his collar in an emergency, he will be used to you doing that and not spook away.

Trainer Leslie Nelson as a great DVD called *Really Reliable Recall*. Find it on her site: http://www.tailsuwin.com/

Dog Reactivity - 11/5/09

Charlie's first dog training class will be this evening so I thought I'd better start working on his dog reactivity issues before I go.

The last two days, I began walking Charlie in town. I thought I might take him into the vet clinic and reward him for being calm around other dogs. I decided against that because the space in the clinic is not large enough to keep a far enough distance away from the other dogs. I didn't want Charlie to feel cramped and scared. I opted instead for walking him around outside in town. I picked a quiet back street. At first he wanted to lunge and drag me. I just kept stopping, helping him get back into a position next to my side and then rewarded him for walking in that position. When he lost focus, I gently turned in the other direction and coaxed him back next to me. I had him target on my hand to bring him back where I wanted rather than leading him with food.

We found a house with a Malamute pup tethered on the front porch. With the owner's permission, I walked Charlie back and forth down the sidewalk in front of the dog. I led Charlie with food the first couple of times to keep his attention away from lunging and barking at the other dog. I didn't want him to rehearse the aggressive behavior I had seen previously at the vet clinics. I never gave him a chance to become highly aroused and start barking.

After just a few passes by the dog, he figured out this new game and trotted next to me heeling like a pro.

We did the same thing yesterday in my client Judy's driveway doing walk-bys with her gorgeous and very big Rhodesian Ridgeback, Sydney. Although Charlie's first impulse is to lunge and growl, I started far enough away so he never did that behavior. In just a few minutes, we were able to pass within about 10 feet of Syd.

16
THE BASICS OF POSITIVE TRAINING

Training Procedures

We're going to be following the same procedure for all the training ideas in this book. We call this positive training because you'll be working with your dog without using training tactics that involve hurting or scaring him. You've already had a bit of practice with the *Don't Eat the Hand That Feeds You*, *Eye Contact*, *May I Touch Your Body?* and *Hand Targeting* games.

For each behavior, we will follow the same sequence:

❖ You'll get the dog to perform the behavior by capturing, free shaping or luring.

❖ Mark the behavior using either the word "yes" or by the "click" of a clicker.

❖ Give the behavior a name or signal once he's offering the behavior consistently.

❖ Work to generalize the behavior by having him practice the behavior in varied settings and with distractions.

Training Tips

You will want to refer to these often so you may want to bookmark this page.

❖ Plan ahead – What do you want the dog to learn? What "cues" do you want to use?

❖ Be "on the dog's program." What is the emotional state of the dog? Are the time and place conducive to learning? Is your dog under social pressure from other humans, dogs, or other outside distractions?

❖ Use small, easily-swallowed food tidbits for treats. For very food-motivated dogs, their normal kibble food can be used. Limit the use of sugary dog "junk food."

❖ Keep training sessions short – three to five minutes can accomplish a lot of training.

❖ Stop when the dog still wants to work.

❖ Have an "on" and an "off" switch for trained behaviors.

❖ Once learned, introduce distractions, distance, and duration for each new behavior.

❖ If the dog gets confused, be ready to back up to reward the dog for a simpler behavior.

❖ Dogs are not good at generalizing. A trick learned in the kitchen may be impossible to perform in the living room! Practice doing behaviors in as many settings as possible. Change your body posture and give the cue. Is your dog relying on more cues to do the trick than you would like?

❖ The dog's latest trick will be his favorite. Be careful about rewarding random "tricks" that the dog throws at you. Ask the dog to perform another behavior, then cue him to do the trick.

❖ Provide yummier treats for more distracting training environments.

❖ Remember, you have your dog for companionship, fun and relaxation. Have fun!

Ways to Get a Behavior

In order to be able to "mark" and reward a behavior, you'll need to somehow get the dog to do the behavior. For example, If you want to teach your dog to "sit," you'll have to figure out a way to get him to bend his back legs and lower his butt to the floor. There are a number of ways you can get a behavior.

❖ **"Modeling"** - You could force the dog into position. This is what many of us learned to do in old fashioned dog training classes. You were supposed to get your dog to sit by pulling up on his neck while pushing down his rump. The obvious question would be, "Would you like someone to teach you a behavior by forcing you to do it?" I know I'd feel resentful and would probably steer clear of my "trainer" in the future. This method has gone the way of the dinosaurs as we've all learned better, more dog friendly training methods.

❖ **"Capturing"** - You could catch the dog doing the behavior and mark the behavior. That's how I've taught my dogs to do cute tricks like bowing or scratching themselves on cue. Once the dog learns that repeating a behavior that you've marked will get him another reward, he'll become adept at learning all sorts of tricks. We call this "capturing" the behavior.

❖ **"Luring"** You could lure the dog into position with a toy or food. This is a very simple way to get the dog to move his body into some positions such as sitting or lying down. There's a problem with luring, however. The dog can get confused and think that the food in your hand is part of the trick. Maybe you've met a dog who only does his tricks when he's following a cookie. So when we use luring as a training tool, we always move the treat to our other hand or another location after a few minutes so the dog can learn to do the behavior without leading him with food.

❖ **"Shaping"** is the term we use for teaching the dog a trick in little steps, marking and rewarding each small step along the way. Free shaping means you're not giving the dog any clues, he's guessing what you want by trying many different behaviors. It's a bit like playing the children's game "Red Light-Green Light."

When I help my clients learn to train their dogs, we use a combination of luring, capturing and shaping. We never force the dog to do behaviors. That way both we and the dog have a good time!

Why You Don't Want to Use Scary Tactics To Train Your Dog

Sue and Pete just can't figure it out. Their once housetrained, calm dog has become psychotic. Dear Suzie is now peeing all over the house, cowers and shakes when the phone rings and goes into an absolute panic when the smoke detector starts tweeting when the battery is getting low.

Sharon's dog Max used to love kids but now growls and lunges when he sees them in the distance.

Fritz the Labrador retriever used to love to play with other dogs. His owner can't figure out why he almost killed a dog at the dog park the last time he was there.

My dog Reggie winces and screams when I throw a ball for him. He cringes when I pour his kibble into his metal food bowl.

Can you guess what these dogs have in common?

Quick fixes are so alluring when you're training your dog. Perhaps you've seen the displays of shock collars and electric fencing systems in your local pet store. Maybe you read a dog training book that suggests that you throw a can of noisy rocks near your dog or spray him with water to get him to stop jumping up and grabbing things off your counter.

The facts is, **when you use scare tactics to attempt to train your dog, you can create problems you may never be able to remedy.**

Let's look at dear Suzie, the once-sweet dog who is now acting psychotic. In recent months, her family decided to install an electric fencing system. They followed the training protocol and taught her that the beep of her collar predicted that she'd get shocked if she proceeded across the property line. That made a big impression on Suzie. She only got shocked a couple of times but, now, has learned to stay within the boundaries of the yard. The problem is that other sounds are now reminding her of the beeping sound of the collar: the cell phone, the smoke detector, the buzzer on the dryer that signals the clothes are dry. Suzie no longer feels safe in the yard either. Last week, she was busy sniffing the trail of a neighbor's dog that wandered through her yard (remember, the electronic fencing doesn't keep the other dog out) and didn't notice she was near the shock zone of the fence. As she trotted over to scent mark on the other dog's urine mark, she got a whopping big shock. She no longer feels safe peeing outside.

You can guess what happened in the other scenarios. Fritz the Lab visited the dog park that is run by the lady who sells shock collars as a training device to teach a perfect recall. Dear Fritz had been shocked a whole year ago while playing with a dog at the park while the owner thought he was training him to come. Instead, Fritz associated the pain of the shock with the presence of the other dog. Now he becomes so anxious and aroused when he sees another dog that he's ready to attack and bite to protect himself from another "shock attack."

Dear Reggie is still scared of throwing motions and the clinking metal sounds

Sharon was worried that Max might overpower kids when she was walking him on a leash, so she'd tighten the leash and jerk Max into a sit position every time a child approached. Now Max gets nervous and defensive even when he sees a kid in the distance.

Reggie's former owners probably followed the advice of one of their friends and rattled or threw a shake can, a can with a few stones in it, to stop behaviors they didn't like when he was a pup. He still gets anxious and scared by sounds and movements that remind him of the scary can.

Aversive training methods, things that are scary to your dog and attempt to suppress his behavior, can always have **fallout** that you may never be able to reverse. Not only that, your dog may generalize his fear to other situations that you never imagined. Is it worth it to you to risk making your dog psychotic in your attempts to train him? Commit to positive reward-based training and management and you'll foster a **relationship that is built on caring and respect rather than fear and suppression**.

Lucy

"Lucy is a very calm, warm and loving dog. Our favorite game to play is *Hide and Seek*. It's fun to hide in the house and say, 'Lucy come!" and watch her run to us with a wagging tail and bright, happy eyes."

The Manning Family

Michigan's' Upper Peninsula 11/17/09

We survived our UP trip despite Charlie's apparent car angst. Pepto-Bismol has become our new traveling companion. I think his tummy kept getting nauseous. He'd sit on the car seat panting and looking out the window. I'd pull off the road and walk him and then resume driving. Soon he'd be doing the strange panting again. I'd then stick $\frac{1}{4}$ of a Pepto-Bismol down his throat and he'd seem able to relax. I will be more observant in the future.

Overall, Charlie was a delightful traveling companion. He was friendly and playful with Margie's dog Tobie and slept peacefully on the bed at night.

He got to spend three days riding in the ranger truck with Dave and me as we passed out wolf information in hunting camps.

I've been working on "stop" and "sit to be leashed." I've also started doing some whistle training and learning to play a toy piano. We're also working on discriminating between a nose touch and a foot touch.

Last evening, Charlie came with me to a meeting at church. We ended up having an impromptu training session – training a cute little kid, Carson, to bravely approach and pet a dog. Charlie did a great job of retrieving.

Frigid Lake Superior on a cold, blustery day

17
SITS, DOWNS & STANDS

We've already talked about teaching your dog a default sit but now we need to get a bit more organized and put his sit behavior on cue. Putting the behavior on cue, or having him do the behavior when you give a specific verbal or hand signal, is a bit of an art. You'll find that most dogs are better at following hand signals than discerning human words. Remember that dogs' wolf ancestors really don't make that many different sounds. At first, it takes quite a bit of brain work for our dogs to differentiate the strange sounds coming out of our mouths.

Young Liam is already an accomplished dog trainer.

First of all, the dog needs to be doing the behavior. You already learned to lure him into a sit with a food treat by holding food in your hand and then moving your hand close over the top of his head until his butt hit the floor, saying "yes" and then rewarding him. I prefer to keep any food lure inside my closed fist rather than have it available for him to lick, grab or paw while I'm doing luring.

The problem with luring any behavior is that the dog may quickly get the idea that the food is part of the trick: "Mom has food in her hand, I follow food, I get rewarded." Many trainers prefer to "free shape" behaviors rather than lure them because they know how confusing luring can be to the dog. For our purposes, luring can be very efficient to train some behaviors as long as we get rid of the food lure as fast as possible.

So, after getting the dog to sit few times using the lure, now put the food in your other hand and make the same hand motion with your *empty* hand. When the dog's butt hits the floor mark the behavior with either a "yes" or a "click" and reward the dog. You now are using your hand motion as a "cue" to get the behavior. If you'd rather have an open hand rather than a closed fist for your cue, flatten your hand and continue to mark and reward your dog each time he sits.

You've already taught your dog how to move from a sit when you practiced *hand targeting.* Now when he's sitting, you can open your flat hand and move it away from him and have him touch it to get him to stand. You can add the cue "stand" once your pup is consistently getting up from the sit when you give him the hand targeting cue. Remember to say the word "stand" and then give your hand targeting cue so he'll learn to listen to your verbal cue word not just follow your hand target.

While you're at it, you may as well teach him a "down." It's easiest to do this by simply luring him from a sit by moving your treat hand toward him between his front legs and toward the back part of his tummy. He'll easily fold down onto the floor.

If you want to try a "down" from a standing position, again move your lure between his front legs and back and he should nicely rock back and fold into a "down."

Remember to quickly switch to using an empty hand rather than a treat-filled one for both of these behaviors or he'll think that the presence of the lure is part of the trick.

Most people also want their dog to respond to spoken cues. When you want to add a word for any trick, you'll want to start *saying* "sit, " down," or "stand" before you make your hand signal cue. If you make your hand signal and say the word at the same time, your dog may never even notice your spoken word. When you say the word before you make your signal the dog will begin to notice the word and anticipate seeing the signal and start responding to your verbal cue.

Now comes the hard part. Remember, dogs don't generalize behaviors as well as we might assume. If your dog learns his new tricks in the kitchen, he may have no idea that you want him to do the same behaviors in the living room. He may be way too distracted at first to do them outside. You'll have to practice any trick in lots of environments with lot of distractions if you want him to do the trick reliably.

Sit and Sit Some More – Building Duration for Sits & Downs

This game teaches your dog to stay in a seated position despite distractions. You will also be able to increase the distance you can get from your dog while he's sitting and increase the amount of time he will stay seated. Once you've practiced doing this game with your dog, you can play the same game with him lying down instead of sitting.

- ❖ Review your pup's basic sit behavior by raising the food-containing hand up and over the pup's head.

- ❖ As soon as the pup's rear hits the floor, say "yes" and reward the dog with a tidbit. Immediately continue to say "yes" to the dog and continue to reinforce him with food in a *"machine gun"* manner. That means keep him in the sitting position by feeding him lots of little treats in quick succession.

❖ Immediately release the dog with a release cue "*Go play*," and turn away from the pup momentarily. "Go play" will become a signal to your dog that you're currently no longer offering any treats.

❖ Again entice the pup into a sit position as before and "machine gun" feed, say "yes" and reward him for just a few more seconds. Release the dog saying, "Go play."

❖ After a few trials, the pup will want to sit. He'll come back over to you and sit in front of you wanting to reengage in the game. He'll be hoping you're going to ask him to sit.

❖ Now add a bit of a distraction, perhaps a gentle foot tap, "Yes" and reward the dog for <u>committing</u> to the sitting position. Release the dog to "go play."

❖ Gradually add new distractions, change your body position, move around, etc. and allow the pup to choose to remain seated. "Yes" and reward the dog each time he commits to maintaining the sit behavior.

❖ Always release the dog from the sit with your "go play" cue.

Now try this same game with your pup doing a "down." Be creative as you practice having your dog stay seated or lying down. Can he do his tricks while you skip around him? How about maintaining his position while you bounce his ball or wave your arms in front of him?

This game is one of the best ways to teach your dog to remain calm in the presence of running, squealing kids. Make a game of having the kids run back and forth while your well-rewarded pup sits calmly amidst the family bedlam!

Buzz loved to chase and grab Liam. Buzz practiced *Sit & Sit Some More* while Liam practiced being a normal hyper kid.

Bell-Ringing – 11/22/09

He did it! Two-hours of bell-ringing like a pro. He didn't show the least bit of fear of shopping carts or rambunctious squealing kids. Not only did he take dollars and stuff them in the bucket like a pro, he was obsessed with using his paw to ring the bells on his "ring-o-matic" (Fisher-Price crib toy retrofitted with hanging bells)

There's a lot to be said for working with a dog that sees the world as a friendly place. Kaddi wanted to come out of the car to ring but then sat there quivering in fear after a few noisy shopping baskets went by. I think she'll be sitting out the season.

Charlie will take the shopper's money and put it in the bucket.

Charlie whopping his "ring-o-matic" with his paw. Our dogs earned over $7,000 bell-ringing in 2009. The dogs had fun and so did we!

18
STUBBORN?

"My dog is stubborn! He just won't do what I say! He should know what to do!" We dog trainers hear this all the time.

I remember many years ago when I was training my Belgian Sheepdog, Jacques. I had been through a couple of traditional dog training classes some years before with other dogs, and had sworn I would never again be a "jerk" trainer. I wanted to use all positive training methods with this new pup. I can still remember the day I was out in the back yard working with him. I wanted him to lie down and he just wouldn't do it. For just a moment, I lapsed back into the trainer I didn't want to be. In frustration, I forcibly pushed him down to the ground. I remember the incident well. I won't forget the look in Jacques eyes. I had betrayed his trust by my impulsive use of force. From that day on, lying down on cue became his least favorite trick.

I've become a much wiser trainer since then. I've given up the use of the word "stubborn" in my training vocabulary and I've come to be much more empathetic with the dogs I train. The biggest problem with using the term "stubborn" to describe your dog is that the word will set you up to somehow think you should make him do something that he doesn't want to do. It will become a matter of your will versus the will of your dog. You'll no longer think of yourselves as working cooperatively together.

How do you feel when someone "makes" you do something? Don't you immediately feel resentful and want to do just the opposite? Can you imagine what our dogs must feel like when we attempt to "make" them comply with our demands?

There are many reasons why your dog might not respond to your cues.

❖ He may not understand what you are asking him to do. Charlie Darwin has a very hard time distinguishing verbal cues. My dear Anja dog excelled at picking words out of sentences and guessing what we were asking of her. Even though she started out as a feral dog living apart from humans, we taught her language, one word at a time as we trained and rewarded her. To her, human speech had meaning. Since we don't really know Charlie's background, except that he was given up to a shelter for being destructive, I'm guessing his former owners spent a lot more time yelling at him than they did training him to respond to verbal cues. To him, most human language still sounds like, "Bla, bla, bla, bla..." with an occasional word he is able to discern.

❖ You may not have taught your dog the trick as well as you thought you did. I thought I had trained puppy Kaddi to make eye contact with me. One day, instead of standing in front of her, I was sitting on the floor. Instead of making eye contact, she was looking up at the angle where my standing body eyes would be. In her understanding, I had been rewarding her for *looking up,* not particularly looking into my eyes!

❖ Your dog may have learned the trick in a specific context. Your dog isn't just hearing the words you're saying when you think you're training him. He's watching your body posture, smelling the aroma of treats in your pocket and noticing all the other small details of the environment. If he learned to do the trick in the kitchen with cookies on the counter, those details may be part of the trick to him. When you move to the living room and the treats are on the mantel, he may not have the slightest idea that you're asking him to do the same behavior for which he was rewarded in the kitchen. You need to help your dog generalize his tricks to lots of settings and learn that your cue is the signal that he can be rewarded for a specific behavior.

❖ The environment may be too distracting or scary for your dog to perform a trick. Being a wild-type village dog, our dear Kaddi gets frightened very easily by things in the environment that most dogs wouldn't even notice. A rotating ceiling fan can look like an attacking monster to her. There's no way she can do her tricks if she's worried about a scary fan.

My trainer friend Chris Bach talks about "being on the dog's program" when you train. You need to be aware of your dog's ability to be teachable. You need to be aware of his sensitivities. Each one of our dogs has a different learning style. Kaddi is very thoughtful and methodical. She can stack the rings on her Fisher-Price™ ring stacking toy. Just don't ask her to do any trick that makes any kind of clanging noise. She winces for fear of the sound of dropping even a ball into a bucket. She has an amazing sense of humor and can turn an agility run into a comedy act; sunbathing on the dog walk and vanishing inside the tunnel while she stops to meditate.

Reggie tries very hard but it takes him a long time to master a new skill. He never offers behaviors on his own. I think he learned that wasn't a safe thing to do in his first home. He's great at copying tricks the other dogs do. He'll watch from a safe distance as they do a trick and then suddenly appear ready to join in the activity.

Lacey is not a dog I wanted or appealed to me in any way. When we first got her from the dog pound, she was spastic, unfocused, destructive, hyperactive and had the attention span of a flea. I literally had to reward her for noticing my attempts to train her one second at a time. She tried my patience, but, luckily, I didn't take her inattentiveness personally. If I moved too fast in my training, she would become sullen and shut down. Lacey is still very sensitive but now, she loves to learn and is a happy, centered dog.

And then there's Charlie. He knows no bounds and is willing to try anything. He's now much less distractible than he was at first. He loves offering behaviors and has definitely figured out how to work the system!

So, what gifts does your dog have? What are his strong points and what areas are going to tax your patience and ability to be a compassionate trainer?

Teaching Your Dog to "Yield to Pressure"

"Stubborn as a mule!" We've all heard that term but have probably never thought of how that expression relates to our dogs. If you're a horse person, you're probably familiar with the concept of "yielding to pressure." What that means is that a well trained horse will move when the slightest pressure is applied to his body. Horses are big and very strong. If you were to try to move a horse with brute strength alone, you'd never get very far. Horse people know that it's important to train their horses to respond willingly to light pressure.

How many times have you seen a dog being walked on a leash and it looks a lot like tug-of-war? How many times have you seen someone trying to lead their dog away from a distraction and the dog is gagging as he's being dragged by the neck? Wouldn't it be nice if your dog would notice the slight pressure on his leash and respond?

Teaching your dog to respond to light pressure on his collar and harness will be easy if you take a bit of time to intentionally teach the behavior.

Start with your dog on a leash attached either to his harness or his collar. Stand in a relaxed body position with the leash in your hand.

Cindy pulls gently on Teddy's harness. She'll say, "yes," or "click," and reward him when he chooses to move toward her. Notice that she's guiding him forward by holding the leash low and straight out rather than pulling up on the leash. Teddy's leash is attached to the front chest ring of his harness.

❖ Gently pull the dog straight forward on the leash. If the dog resists, plants his feet solidly and doesn't move, don't say or do anything. Continue to have even pressure on the leash without tugging the dog. Wait the dog out.

- ❖ The second the dog moves forward, "click" and reward the dog.

- ❖ Repeat this process until the dog will easily move forward with the slightest pull on the leash. Make sure you are applying pressure to pull the dog forward, not pulling up on the leash.

- ❖ Once the dog is responding consistently to your light pull, experiment with moving your dog from one side to the other of your body. Remember to "click" and reward your dog for each movement.

Practice moving the dog with gentle pressure in the house in a quiet environment. Then gradually work on this trick in more distracting environments. Make sure to "click" and reward as you train.

You can expand your dog's sensitivity to pressure on his leash by teaching him to back-up when you gently pull backwards, to sit when you gently pull up and to lie down with slight downward pressure. You'll be amazed at how much more responsive your dog is if you teach him this trick!

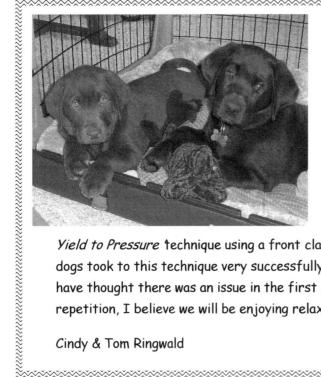

Teddy & Reagan

Yield to Pressure

"What a Difference!! Both Reagan and Teddy fought the leash, they didn't want to move, or they tugged in the opposite direction. I was concerned about how we were going to fix this problem without dragging or jerking their necks.

Yield to Pressure technique using a front clasp harness was the answer. Both dogs took to this technique very successfully and immediately. You never would have thought there was an issue in the first place. With a continual training and repetition, I believe we will be enjoying relaxing and rewarding walks in no time."

Cindy & Tom Ringwald

19
BECOMING RELEVANT TO YOUR DOG

You open the door, the dog barges out. You open the door, the dog barges in…..

Has your dog even noticed that you're the one attached to the door?

Often an impediment to training is that your dog is getting his cues more from the environment than he is from you. You may think he's learned your signals but instead he's keying off other factors, not your words or presence. One of the magical routes to a great companion dog is to have the dog become aware of and respond to the cues _you_ give, to help the dog learn that the funny garbled sounds that he hears coming from your mouth have meaning to how he gets what he wants.

Often people become more relevant to their dogs in negative ways rather than positive ones. The dog may learn that the presence of a person inhibits him from doing or getting what he wants. Perhaps the presence of a person makes it unsafe to grab things off the counter or chase the cat or relieve himself. He learns that the presence of a person can be scary or inhibit his enjoyment of life.

So, much of our training becomes finding ways to insert ourselves into our dog's life so our communication with him or the "cues" we give to him become relevant to him in a positive way.

An example is my dog Reggie. He came from a home where he learned that the best way to live safely around the humans in his household was to keep out of their way. The people were not abusive although I do suspect they may have used scary methods of inhibiting his behavior such as a throw can with noisy coins or stones in it. His owners apparently didn't do any systematic training with Reggie. They didn't spend time teaching him basic cues like sit or down. Instead, he learned to watch for signs in the environment that made sense to him and helped him get by without getting into trouble. So a human near a door meant go outside or come back in. What the human said near the door had no relevance to him. He had not learned that discriminating anything about human speech made any difference in how his world worked.

So, how do we help our dogs to insert us into their worlds – to make ourselves relevant to them?

- ❖ First, systematically teach basic behaviors through positive training methods. You can't expect your dog to sit at the door before you let him out if you haven't practiced the behavior with the cue ("sit" and/or hand signal) in a less distracting environment.

- ❖ Start inserting the trained behaviors into contexts so the dog has to respond to the cues before he gets what he wants. "Do you want to go outside? OK, you need to sit first" or "Do you want me to play tug with you? You'll have to lie down first."

Be patient. Old habits and tricks die hard. You will need to be the rewarding part of your dog's environment. Little by little you'll see him watching you more and looking for cues from you. Your relationship will grow and the two of you will have a better life together!

Charlie waiting to go outside
He has to sit before I open the door. I may send
him out to chase a squirrel and then reward him for
coming back.

The sock – 11/30/09

I'm musing this morning about the sock. I was reading in bed this morning when Charlie was becoming antsy. He'd already been outside a couple of times and was probably trying to let me know he was hungry.

He started rummaging around the bedroom. First he was eating a Kleenex and then showed interest in my sock. I continued to read. A few minutes later, I noticed he was dissecting something about 10 feet away just out of the room - my sock!!

I'm starting to put together a picture of the dog who was taken to the pound and given up, knowing full well that they were sending him to certain death.

Charlie is a very smart little guy who knew some tricks that served him well but drove his previous owners beyond their limits. He knows how to get attention by grabbing and mangling objects (socks, pens, etc.) that smell like their owner. He knows how to flatten himself to go under a fence. I'm sure he had a great time playing the "na-na-na-na-na. you can't catch me" game and the "na-na-na-na-na. I've got something of yours and you'll never get it back" game....

He still has bladder control issues. When we left the dogs in the house while our neighbor came to pick up the rest of our goat supplies (Blue Bell has moved down the street to her new home), we came back inside to find marks of a urine stream that stretched through the entire living room and kitchen. He was obviously running in circles and peeing at the same time.

So how do I react to these unwanted behaviors?

The fence is now pushed down close to the ground and no longer entices Charlie to go under. The peeing will have to be managed. I'll keep his belly band close at hand to use when I think he might have an accident or if I'm taking him somewhere that would be a horrific place to pee.

The stealing and dissecting will need to be managed carefully. For sure, I don't want to reward the behavior by jumping up and feeding the guy or encouraging a game of keep-away. I have two options for now. This morning, I quietly got up and walked him to his crate. In his dog mind, the reward for sock dissecting is his crate rather than my attention or a game. Probably not the reward he was hoping to get. My other option is to watch for his "communication" behavior in the morning when he's trying to get my attention and teach him to bring something to me that would then be rewarded. I'm thinking I'll teach him to bring his food bowl and then reward him with some yummies in it.

Charlie is modeling his belly band in this photo. It's an elasticized cloth band that Velcos ™ around his waist and is made to hold a sanitary napkin or other absorbent material. Belly bands work great for male dogs that are incontinent or have become used to marking indoors. I ordered Charlie's at http://www.bellybands.net/.

20
PUPPY MANAGEMENT

"Bum habits are hard to break"

Good dog trainers know it's a lot easier to prevent problems than to let the pup develop bad habits and then try to fix them later.

Here are some management tricks to do with your pup:

1. **Keep a drag line on your pup** – a 6' cord should work just fine in the house and a lightweight longer rope or lunge line outdoors. This line will help you:

    ❖ Keep from scaring your pup by running at him and grabbing him when he's house soiling or running away with something that you don't want him to have. You can step on the line and approach quietly and gently and help him to move to an appropriate spot to relieve himself or practice the *Bad Dog Retrieve* (Chapter 22) to help him learn how to bring you things rather than steal them from you and chew them up.

    ❖ Practice calling him away from distractions and rewarding him. When possible, help him come away and then send him back to "go play" again. You will be able to preventing the "you can't catch me" game.

2. **Keep tantalizing food items out of range** – Keep your pup from developing counter surfing skills. If he's very interested in something on the table or counter, practice calling him away and rewarding a sit instead.

3. **Don't play games or practice tricks with your pup that will haunt you later on** – Some examples of games that you will wish your dog never learned:

    ❖ Chasing & grabbing kids, kitties or bicycles, lawnmowers or cars

    ❖ Barking for cookies or to get your attention

- ❖ Thinking he can crawl up your body to get close to you

- ❖ Jumping at the door and barking to be let out or in

- ❖ Playing tug games with clothing, garden hoses or other things that are not toys

- ❖ Table begging

- ❖ Dragging humans while on leash

4. **Mindfully install good manners and skills that will last a lifetime**

- ❖ Sit and wait at doors

- ❖ Default "leave it" – Your dog won't automatically dive for any food morsel or interesting item he sees. (see the *Walk Away Game, Don't Eat the Hand that Feeds You* and *"Leave It,"* (Chapter 25)

- ❖ Lie down on mat (See the *Mat Game,* Chapter 27)

- ❖ Quiet dogs get cookies, get let outside, and are allowed out of their crates

Share these guidelines with all family members and visitors to your home so your pup is treated *consistently* or he will learn to test boundaries and you will create a sneaky, pushy monster instead of a joyful compliant friend.

Sit to be Petted - 12/8/09 -

It's time to expand Charlie's talents. We've been bell-ringing a bunch of times and he's doing phenomenally well. Now it's time to get more organized about sitting and staying with distractions. I've been doing some work on having him wait while I walk ahead on the road (with him on a long line) and then either going back to him or calling him to me from the *wait.* I also practiced a bit of stay on the mat while my friends were working their dogs at our impromptu training time we had together a few days ago.

Yesterday, I decided it was time to start working on a formal "sit to be petted" routine. Left to his own devices, Charlie bounces, climbs on people and occasionally grabs at hands. (Check out *Sit to be Petted* for the details) This morning, I expanded the game to include touching his front feet and ears. He'll have to be handled this way for the Canine Good Citizen test so we may as well start practicing already.

It's supposed to snow later. Time to find a sledding harness to get ready for the season!

Charlie is looking very civilized practicing his new *Sit to be Petted* trick. He used to jump all over people when they attempted to pet him.

Sledding can be great winter entertainment for you and your dogs.

21
CRATES, CONFINEMENT, POOPS & HUMAN SANITY

Wouldn't it be grand if your new dog could move into your house and only chew on his own toys, be perfectly housebroken, and able to lie quietly at home for long hours while you're away? Wouldn't it be wonderful to never have to go anywhere so you could spend all your time watching your new pup? It's not going to happen, is it?

To keep from hating your new pup, you're going to have to be realistic about how long it takes to have a calm, mature, housebroken, and non-destructive dog. You're going to have to be wise puppy managers so your pup can mature into that fantasy pet. Because you can't be there constantly to monitor your pup's behavior, you're going to have to come up with some safe ways to contain him when you aren't able to watch him. Left to his own devices, he's going to eliminate wherever he wants to and chew up whatever he can fit into his mouth.

Dogs must think we're pretty crazy. We get to eliminate inside while we throw a hissy fit when they do the same! I know you've heard that dogs are "den" animals that would never soil their own living quarters, but that just isn't true. Wolf pups only live in a den for a few short weeks and, by the time they're adults, wolves have been shown to scent mark as much as 30 times an hour while traveling through their territory. So when we attempt to "housetrain" our dogs, we really are expecting a lot from them. It's going to take a lot of patience and consistency to help them to learn to eliminate when and where we find it appropriate.

Puppies learn by exploring their environment the way they know best: they tug, shred, disembowel and maybe even eat anything they can fit in their mouths. For his own safety and for the safety of your personal belongings, you're going to have to be very diligent in monitoring which items are "explored" by your pup.

So, to keep from hating your new pup, you're going to need some assistance and lots of patience. Here are some tools that will help along the way:

❖ **Puppy Godparents:** No, you can't stuff your new pup in the laundry room or a crate and disappear for the whole day and not expect unwanted consequences. Your puppy needs social

113

interaction. He also will need to relieve himself often. There's a formula that can give you a ballpark figure for the amount of time your pup may be able to go without needing to relieve himself: take his age in months and add 1 to get the approximate number of hours between potty breaks. If you work long hours, you'll need to have someone else to care for your dog when you can't be there to care for him. You could hire a professional dog sitter or maybe you have a neighbor who can help out.

> Learn the basics of positive housetraining methods by selecting a book from http://www.dogwise.com

❖ **A good quality carpet cleaning machine:** Nothing will make you hate your dog faster than cleaning vomit, slushy poop or urine out of your new carpeting. Plan ahead. Before you get your pup, spend part of your doggie layette money on a good quality carpet cleaning machine. Remember, you don't want to be screaming at your dog when he's peeing all over your living room. All that will teach him is to find a safer place to relieve himself next time, maybe behind the couch or in the back room! You always want to be "safe" to your dog, not "dangerous."

❖ **Odor neutralizer:** Everyplace your pup has an "accident" will smell like a bathroom to him in the future. Buy a good quality odor neutralizer to destroy, not only mask, the odor.

❖ **A crate or other safe form of confinement:** You've got to have a safe place to keep your new dog when you're unable to monitor his behavior both for his safety and the protection of your belongings. Most likely, your dog will be able to have freedom in your house once he's thoroughly housetrained and over his puppy chewing but, until then, control his wandering.

Can your dog love his crate?

The biggest mistake a harried puppy owner can make is to stuff her new puppy in a crate without taking some time to acclimate the pup slowly. After all, how would you feel if someone stuffed you into a tiny cell and then vanished from sight? Puppies that are forced to cope with being locked into a crate without some positive training often develop symptoms of separation anxiety later on.

Dogs can be trained to *love* their crates. I think the best crate training demo I've ever seen is done by trainer Susan Garrett. I'm only going to explain a few important ideas here, but I highly recommend that you buy Susan's video and work through her crate games. They are superb!

Charlie loves his crate. For him, it's a great place to chew a pork hide bone or wait for goodies to appear.

❖ Your dog needs to learn to be separated from you little by little whether as a pup in a crate or an older dog left alone at home. You never want him to panic in your absence. He's most apt to be upset when you first leave, so give him something to keep him busy. You can soak his kibble dinner and mash it into a rubber Kong™ toy and freeze it. That will keep your pup busy during the first minutes of separation. This will help prevent departure barking. You don't want to be the owner of a dog who gets you in trouble with your neighbors for non-stop barking when you're gone.

❖ Practice having your dog "sit" when in his crate. An easy method is to pull the crate pan from the crate and practice "sits" outside of the crate on the pan. Then put the pan back into the crate and practice the trick there.

❖ Now, practice only opening the crate door if the dog sits first. <u>Never</u> open the crate door while the dog is standing, barking, whining, pawing, or bouncing. His *quiet* sitting behavior will be rewarded when you open the door and invite him out.

> Trainer Susan Garrett has made a wonderful video about crate training your dog. To order it, go to: http://www.clickerdogs.com/crate_games.php

❖ Another crate training trick you can do is lock one of his favorite chewies inside the crate. Have him practice sitting to wait to go back into the crate to chew on it.

Charlie knows to sit when I put my hand on the cage latch. He then waits for me to invite him out.

Charlie, DSA - 12/13/09

Yippee – Charlie is now a Dog Scout!!! Our dear friend Maggie who is a Dog Scout evaluator came to help us bell-ring for the Salvation Army. She's had hours to watch dear Charlie as he gaily charges up to people to take their money and put it in the bucket. She's watched him greet hundreds of people and happily bash his bells with his paw. All that is nice, but to become a scout, he had to have a formal test. He was able to do the required behaviors, sit, down, stay, come, walk on a loose leash, and "leave it" with food. As his Mom, I had to answer a bunch of questions about how I understood being "the smart end of the leash."

I am proud and happy!! Now Charlie will be able to wear a Dog Scout kerchief when working in public and start qualifying for DSA badges.

Charlie B. Darwin, DSA

22
THE BAD DOG RETRIEVE

Dogs' brains seem to come pre-programmed to play two games especially made to drive their owners crazy. One game is the "you can't catch me game" and the other is "I've got something of yours that I'm never giving back and you can't catch me" game. Isn't it amazing that your puppy can find your most valuable things to steal and chew up?

Actually, your dog's brain comes wired to watch your eyes to see what you're looking at. Have you ever noticed what pretty yellow eyes dogs' wolf ancestors have? When wolves are hunting in a pack, not only are they good at giving social signals to each other with their eye movements but they're quick to notice what another wolf is looking at. If one wolf is keyed in on chasing a specific elk, the rest of the pack can notice what he's looking at and join in the chase.

If you've ever had the experience of having two human toddlers in a room with a bunch of toys, you know that whatever one of the kids decides to play with, the other kid wants too. Puppies are the same way. If, let's say, your puppy picks up your best fluffy slipper and you charge over and rip it out of his mouth, you have now made the forbidden slipper worth a million dog dollars to your dog. He wants it even more because you wanted it from him so badly. I'm convinced that dogs make mental lists of all the things you've grabbed from them (see *How to Make Your Dog Sneaky*). When you're not around to police those possessions, your dog is going to start compulsively going down his list and grabbing and chewing as many of those things as he can. Sometimes, what some owners think is separation anxiety (their dog eats forbidden objects when they're not at home), is really the dog making up for lost time grabbing all the things his owners have been guarding from him.

Charlie with a very fuzzy slipper
If I were to yell and make a big deal about him having it, it would become worth a million dog dollars and he'd want it even more.

So, in summary:

- ❖ Dogs love to steal items and start a game of keep-away.

- ❖ Any item that is in the possession of another dog is valued.

- ❖ When an owner runs at a dog grabbing an item from the dog and "growling" (yelling), the value of the item increases to the dog.

- ❖ Items that become valued during the formative puppy months may have increased value throughout the dog's life.

Practice the *Bad Dog Retrieve* and your dog will bring you your cherished items rather than sneaking away with them to chew them up.

Many owners consider their dogs "bad" when, in fact they can use this behavior to positively train a reliable retrieve. Follow these steps and you will get a dog who is willing to retrieve just about anything. My dear Anja dog became an expert at retrieving food items. She'd even bring me a hotdog or a cooked chicken breast.

Phase I.

1. When a dog has an item that you do not want him to have, approach slowly, preferably sideways, rather than head-on. Step on your puppy's drag line to make it impossible for him to run off with the item in his mouth.

2. Do not look at the coveted item.

3. Praise the dog saying, "Good Dog, Good hold it!"

4. Gently grasp the coveted item with one hand and slip a valued treat into the dog's mouth behind the item.

5. The dog will sense the food in his mouth and start moving his jaws to eat it.

6. Say, "thank you," and gently remove the item, immediately feeding him another very yummy treat.

7. Immediately offer the item back to the dog, saying, "Take it."

8. After the dog again grasps the coveted item repeat steps 3-5

9. Offer the item again, repeating the procedure.

10. Put the coveted item out of the dog's reach for the time being and play with the dog with another toy or do some other activity that is rewarding to the dog.

Did you notice something strange in this procedure so far? What most people do is "trade" the forbidden item with a treat or another toy as quickly as they can. Dogs wise up to this deception very fast and become very cagey about giving up prized possessions. This also puts the owner in a bind to continually find higher value treats or toys with which to trade. In the *Bad Dog Retrieve* we are immediately giving the forbidden object back to the dog. He won't have time to crunch or chew it because you'll be slipping the food into the back of his mouth and removing the item right away.

Phase II.

1. Arm yourself with delectable items and a previously coveted item.

2. Approach the dog offering the item and say, "Take it."

3. Praise the dog for grabbing the item. Then immediately "trade" the food morsel for the item and practice the "thank you" trick.

4. Offer, trade, and treat a few more times, practicing the "take it," "hold it," "thank you" sequence.

5. Put the item on the floor in front of the dog and ask the dog to "take it" from the floor.

6. Start tossing the item a short distance and reward the dog lavishly for approaching you to trade for the goodies. If you think there is any chance the dog might "snatch and run" do this entire sequence on leash. You may like to add "pick it up" and "bring it" cues at this point.

7. Put the item up and move on to another fun activity with the dog.

Phase III.

Practice the above sequence but now substitute varied items of different size, weight, texture, and shape.

Results

❖ Your dog will be able to hold and retrieve a variety of items.

❖ Your dog may bring you items rather than take off with them.

❖ Stealing and chewing will be replaced with retrieving and holding behaviors.

So, remember, no running and screaming after your dog when he grabs something you don't want him to destroy. Relax, go get high quality treats, and use his interest in carrying things to your training advantage. You'll be surprised how well this works!

Yes, I'll even trust Charlie to hold my camera! Now, if I could just teach him how to take nice pictures!

Does he really get it? - 12/29/09

It's been a busy month and a half – lots of Salvation Army bell-ringing. Charlie has proven himself to be a hard worker. He's spent over 30 hours in the past weeks standing in front of Wal-Mart ringing his bells and grabbing dollars from shoppers' hands and stuffing them in a bucket.

I've created a bell-ringing monster! Dear Charlie has received thousands of treats for whopping the bells with his front foot and grabbing money from people's hands. It would have been ideal to be very organized about this, giving him a cue each time and then marking and rewarding his behavior. I fantasized having him return to "heel" position between each behavior or having him sit quietly for petting. Instead, it was often sheer pandemonium with Charlie ringing often with no reward, shoppers petting him at the same time he's taking money, Charlie staring at approaching friendly persons rather than looking at me for direction. Not a scenario of organized training!

I guess I shouldn't have been at all surprised when a couple of days ago, Charlie's response to my trained cues had turned into random mish-mash of guessing and doing just about any behavior for any cue. I asked him to "sit" and he lay down. I asked him to lie down and he started batting things with his paw. When I took him for a walk, his focus was just about everywhere else but on me.

So, it's time to regroup and get back to being organized about training. Charlie wasn't misbehaving, he was just confused by all the random signals he's been given over the past weeks.

Despite all this poor communication with him, he's come a long way into fitting into our lives. He's great with all our dogs. Even Kaddi, who is the queen of being grumpy, not only tolerates him but is relaxed when he's on the bed next to her. She runs and plays with him outdoors, and occasionally has a wrestle romp with him in the house.

He's still ripping corners off what's left of his foam bed when he gets bored in his crate when we're away. But, overall, he's a pretty easy guy to live with. I have to watch him most in the mornings when I'm checking in on my computer stuff. In his past life, he apparently learned to get people's attention by grabbing and chewing on their belongings. If I'm intently working on the computer, I need to keep one ear open for the sounds of eating pens or chewing on other non-toy items. So far, the *Bad Dog Retrieve* has saved him from sneaky stealing and chewing behavior. If he picks up a non-toy item (like a dropped pen), I can call him over and reward him for retrieving it.

He's still somewhat hesitant about getting into the car. A few times, he's stood over in the field while I'm loading up the other dogs. I've then walked up to him and rewarded him and called him to come with me rather than giving him the chance to be evasive.

The *Bad Dog Retrieve* has helped our dogs collect thousands of dollars for charity

23
PUPPY BEHAVIOR CHART

Here's a fun chart that will remind you how important it is for you to be proactive in training your dog. Your dog is always learning, whether you're influencing that learning or not. Left to his own devices, most of the things he learns are going to drive you crazy and most likely get your dog into trouble. Enjoy!

Puppy Behavior	Puppy Interpretation	Human Interpretation	Long-Range Outcome without Remediation	Training Protocol
Puppy doesn't come when called	Screaming people are scary. Playing chase with people is fun. Why stop when I'm having a good time?	Puppy disobeys Dog should know what to do	Dog unsafe off leash, Unapproachable and uncatchable when loose	Teach recall NEVER chase puppy Keep puppy on drag line
Puppy soils in house	I've got to go NOW! It's scary outside, and safer to go inside. I have stomach cramps and just have to go! What's their problem anyway, they get to pee & poop in the house, besides the house smells like pee and poop!	Puppy disobeys Puppy is mad about something and doing this intentionally	Dog is never fully housetrained Dog may have learned it's unsafe to relieve himself near humans and gets sneaky about where he goes	Feeding schedule Quality food Stool check for parasites and/or bacterial overgrowth Confinement Consistent potty place & schedule Rewards for pottying outside

Puppy Behavior	Puppy Interpretation	Human Interpretation	Long-Range Outcome without Remediation	Training Protocol
Puppy grabs hands & clothing	What fun! Let's play tug the human Human hands are scary - I'm going to bite those scary hands before they get me	Puppy playing In extreme cases – puppy aggressive	Dog outgrows puppy chewing Dog becomes master of harassing humans – possibly biting	Teach non-aggressive play Channel energy to safe play Do not allow bullying play Reward body handling
Puppy grabs non-toy items	What fun! These things must be worth a lot if my people want them so much.	Dog is diabolical at stealing and destroying their stuff Puppy is doing this intentionally	Dog has fun trashing stuff Unsafe to leave the dog alone	"Puppy-proof " house *Bad Dog Retrieve* – teach the pup that bringing objects is more rewarding than stealing them and eating them elsewhere
Puppy barks at strangers	New people are scary New people are exciting	Wow! Look how my puppy is protecting me	Dog has aggression problems toward people	Increase socialization - the presence of strangers predicts yummy rewards
Puppy growls & guards his toys or food	I am scared someone will steal my stuff	He likes to protect his belongings I am scared of my dog when he acts like this	Dog gets good at chasing people away from things Dog snaps at or bites people when they get close to his belongings.	Practice rewarding human approach Socialization *Mine!* Protocols (see bibliography) Practice calling dog away from enticing objects and rewarding him

Puppy Behavior	Puppy Interpretation	Human Interpretation	Long-Range Outcome without Remediation	Training Protocol
Puppy pees during greetings	I am insecure meeting people	My dog gets too excited when he meets new people	Dog continues to pee	Teach humans non aroused greeting, build pup's confidence with new humans through rewards
Pup rolls on back and becomes motionless or greets people by groveling	I am insecure with people, I am diffusing their aggression	Pup is accepting owner as "Alpha" Pup is guilty about something	Dog continues to display submissive behaviors to appease humans	Build dog's confidence through training and positive interaction
Pup wiggles and tries to get away when restrained Puppy grabs at hands trying to pet him	I don't like this, I'm scared, Help!	Pup is being "dominant"	Dog learns to bite to protect himself	Positive handling exercises *May I Touch Your Body?*
Puppy pulls and lunges when walking on leash	Help! They're trying to choke me! Pup is scared, especially if he's on a collar that is hurting or constricting his neck Hey, I want to go this way instead! Wow! Pulling people around is lots of fun!	Pup is disobeying	Owners let their dog drag them around Owners resort to painful control collars Owners stop trying to walk their dogs	Reward –based leash training Awareness of dog's fears and sensitivities Indirect access training

Pogo

In-House Foraging for Dogs

"When Pogo, a rescue doodle from IDOG, acquired me, he came with a reputation for intelligence and talents in 'dissecting' people's possessions. At first I fed him his breakfast in a bowl before I left for work. He inhaled the food in a couple of minutes or less and then, a high point in the day was over. He'd be left alone with time on his paws for interior redecorating. At first, I crated him while I was away, but as I observed him -- it's crucial to observe your dog throughout its life in order to understand it --I came up with various enrichment plans which mean that Pogo is seldom ever crated. Dr. Ian Dunbar says that food bowls for dogs can deprive dogs and owners of opportunities to come up with creative ways for dogs to earn their food. One way they can earn food is by foraging. Long story short, I used Pogo's talents to give him a job: in-house foraging for breakfast. Measuring out his various foods for the day, I put his breakfast in Kongs, bones, and hooves and place them around the house, also sprinkling kibble here and there. By using little dabs of cheese and peanut butter, as well as Pet Botanics, jerky, freeze dried meat, in bones, Kongs, or hooves, I can put out a lot of chewy objects for him to locate. Sprinkling kibble here and there also gives him more to pick up, increasing the time he spends foraging for his breakfast. He typically takes 20 – 50 minutes, depending on how challenging I make the Kongs, bones, or hooves. He's maintained his weight between 35 and 40 pounds for several years, a weight which his vet finds very acceptable – and he has nice white teeth too!"

Pat Goodmann
Senior Wolf Handler, Wolf Park

24
THE WALK AWAY GAME

I thank my friend Chris Bach and her Third Way™ training for first teaching me this wonderful game. Most dogs are naturally extremely impulsive. If they see something they'd like to eat, grab or chase, they tend to become complete lizards. You might call them and they seem to be deaf or, if they're on a leash, they just about rip your arm out of its socket trying to drag you to whatever interests them.

This game teaches the dog to, in Chris' terms, "relinquish the environment" as a default behavior. You become more rewarding than the stuff the dog is trying to get to. I know this sounds impossible, but this game really works. If you practice this game in a variety of settings, your dog will be a thinking Einstein in the presence of distractions.

Here's what you do:

❖ Arm yourself with two kind of treats. One that the dog will die for, maybe a bit of cooked chicken or other doggie delicacy, and the other, a cookie that is at least about an inch long.

❖ Start out with the pup on his leash attached to the chest ring of his harness. Your dog will have a much harder time thinking if there's pressure on his throat from a collar.

❖ Holding tightly on the leash, drop the enticing cookie just out of reach of the pup. Make absolutely sure that the dog cannot access the food that is dropped.

❖ Let the pup attempt to get the food. Do not say anything. Wait. **Do not do anything.**

❖ The second the pup changes his focus from the food to you, say "yes" or "click" your clicker and give your dog a very high value treat from your hand.

❖ Repeat until the dog no longer lunges at the food but automatically turns toward you when the food is dropped.

❖ Now start working to walk past the food on the floor. The instant the pup changes his focus from the food, say "yes" and reward the dog. Continue to reward the dog as he responds and moves away from the enticing cookie on the floor.

❖ Repeat this sequence until the dog can walk past the food on a loose leash and choose to leave it alone.

Practice this game often. Try increasing the value of the item you put on the floor. Maybe you can try walking past a piece of pizza or a hamburger. If your dog wants to chase your cat, you can play "walk away from Kitty." Outside, on a walk, you can practice the fine art of walking past the barking dogs in your neighbors' yards. You can reward your dog for walking past puddles if he's a water crazed retriever, or past a herd of tennis balls if he's a ball addict.

As you can probably guess, this little game is going to become an invaluable part of training your dog to walk nicely on a leash. It's also going to help him to bring himself away from Lizard brain to Einstein.

Aunt Beth's Yummy Tuna Cookies

In a blender, puree:

1 12oz can of tuna packed in water. Do not use White Albacore Tuna as it has higher levels of mercury. Do not drain the tuna.

¼ cup water (or whatever you need to get the tuna blended)

2 TBS Cornstarch

Dump into a bowl.

Add enough Cream of Wheat Cereal (original flavor – no sugar added) to make a sticky dough.

Place small round balls about ½-3/4" in diameter on your microwave's glass dish.

Flatten with a fork like peanut butter cookies.

Microwave approximately 1 ½ minutes per side.

The cookies should be somewhat rubbery. Store them in the freezer in an airtight container or freezer bag.

This same recipe can be modified using canned Salmon. Wild caught is healthier than farm-raised.

Scooter & More - 1/9/10

We all teared up as Charlie rode Anja's scooter for the first time on Thursday for my program at the library. This little guy has lived here less than a few months and he's already doing things that I took years to train with my other dogs.

The scooter is a case in point. I didn't even show it to Anja for the first year I had it. I knew she'd flip out. She was so scared of new things. I got her used to it over a period of weeks and finally was able to get her to ride it. Then it became one of her favorite tricks.

The difference with Charlie is that he's not frightened of new things. I learned so much by painstakingly dealing with Kaddi, Reggie and Lacey's fears. They've all made me the trainer I am today. It's a breath of fresh air to be training a dog who doesn't always worry about whether the sky is falling. I may become spoiled by this dog!

Charles is now learning to come and bother me Lassie-style when he's bored. When I'm working at the computer, he's putting his cute little paws on my lap and staring into my eyes. While I'm honored that he's becoming connected enough with me to come to actively seek my attention, I'm seeing the pitfalls of this behavior "working" for him. I really don't want to have a dog that bugs me for attention. If I let this behavior work part of the time, I'm going to end up with my attention giving being an intermittent reward, the strongest kind, and Charlie will become thoroughly obnoxious.

So, I'm going to commit to having a dog mat near where I work. When Charlie comes looking for attention, I'm going to put the mat down and start rewarding Charlie intermittently for lying on the mat quietly. That trick will make it easier to take Charlie new places and have him look like a well-trained dog!

25
"LEAVE IT!"

Now that your pup is an expert at walking past cookies, kitties, wastebaskets or whatever you used to play the *Walk Away Game*, it's time to make this even more fun by teaching him the cue "leave it" so he'll be able to resist just about any temptation. I say "just about any" because I did have to pry a very tasty brownie out of Charlie's mouth last evening while we were collecting donations at a concert at the opera house in town!

Not only can "leave it" be a fun trick, but it can be a lifesaver for your dog. How many dogs do you know that can catch a food scrap falling from the kitchen counter before it hits the ground? What if, instead of a food scrap, a bottle of prescription meds bounced on the floor in front of your dog? Your "leave it" could save you a costly trip to the vet to have his stomach pumped!

To start this game, you'll want to be sitting on the floor with your dog in a "down" position in front of you. You are going to be using skills he's already learned; just making them a bit more refined.

- ❖ Put your flat open hand on the floor with a treat underneath it about a foot in front of your dog. Say nothing. Your dog may claw at your hand. If necessary, move your hand a few more inches away or, in extreme cases (I had to do this with Kaddi), put a protective garden glove on your hand.

- ❖ Wait until the dog stops mugging your hand and looks up at you. Say "yes," or "click," and then give the dog a small treat from your other hand.

- ❖ Repeat this sequence a few times until your dog automatically looks at you when you put the food on the floor in front of him with your hand covering it.

Buzz working on the beginning of *Leave It!* Just like in *the Walk Away* game, I'll wait for him to look at me away from the food before I "click" and reward him.

- ❖ Now, start to raise your hand a bit above the food, but still have your hand close enough to the cookie so you can cover the food if your dog should make a quick lunge for it. Say, "yes," or "click," when your dog chooses to look at you instead of the food.

- ❖ Now, add the cue "Leave-it" as you place your hand covering the treat on the floor. Say, "Yes," or "click," when the dog looks at you instead of the hand covering the treat.

- ❖ Repeat the cue "leave-it" and start raising your hand above the food. As you feel comfortable, move your hand farther and farther away from the food. Always "click" and reward when he looks at you instead of the food.

- ❖ Always pick up the treat from the floor rather than telling your dog to, "get it," otherwise, your dog may become obsessed with guessing when you're going to give him a cue to grab the food.

Buzz is mesmerized by the cookie on the floor but getting better at leaving it alone

Dogs seem to love this game once they catch on. Usually, I'm able to balance cookies on a dog's forelegs in the first session of playing this game. You'll have to think of your own variations to help your dog generalize this game into lots of settings. Here are some ideas:

- ❖ Have your dog leave a piece of pizza on a plate on a coffee table.

- ❖ Try "extreme leave-it" by piling dog cookies all around your dog.

The next more advanced stage of this game will be the "dropped goodie" leave it. You will be teaching your dog how to leave something that you've dropped on the floor. Think of how many times you accidentally drop things from your kitchen counter. Dogs quickly learn to pounce on dropped items. However, what if you dropped a prescription pill -- something that could be fatal to your dog if he were to eat it? Teaching your dog this trick could save his life!

You'll teach this trick one step at a time so he knows each step well before you proceed to the next.

- ❖ Start by sitting next to your dog on the floor. Instead of saying "Leave it" and placing the cookie near him, *drop* the cookie from a few inches above the floor. Watch out; your well-trained dog might be ready to grab the cookie. Dropping it is a whole new trick. Be prepared to cover the cookie with your hand or foot if he tries to lunge for it. Be sure to "click" and reward when he looks away from the cookie and makes eye contact with you.

If you feel a bit unsure a4bout your dog's ability to forego jumping at the cookie, back up and practice his earlier leave-it game a bit more. If you're still feeling a bit queasy about doing this advanced work, put his harness on, attach his leash to the back ring and tether him to an immovable object. Many people think they need to *bark* the "leave it" cue as a command. You're not trying to scare your dog away from the food; you're teaching him a positively trained trick, so say your "leave it" cue in a normal tone of voice.

❖ Gradually increase the height from which you drop the cookie. When you can drop it from about three feet and he remains calm and looks at you, you are ready to move on to the next step.

Now move into your kitchen. If your dog is already used to grabbing falling food scraps mid-air, you may want to tether him for extra safety.

❖ Again, ask him to "leave it" and drop the goodie. Be certain to reward him each time he is successful -- that will be *every* time, since you're not going to let him make a mistake.)

❖ Practice, practice, practice. Work to be able to say the "leave it" cue *while* the food is still dropping, and finally, to say "Leave it" after the food has been dropped.

You'll be surprised; soon your dog will be doing an "implied" leave it, when something drops. He'll look to you rather than diving for the morsel.

Remember, this is a fun game, but it can be a lifesaver if you drop something that's toxic to your dog. Practice this game often so it becomes one of your dog's favorite tricks.

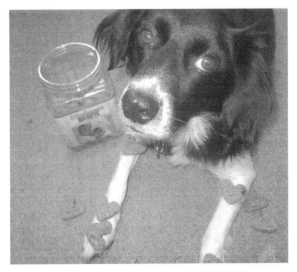

Charlie practicing "Extreme Leave-It!" with his favorite healthy dog cookies. The more you practice this game, the more skilled your dog will become!

How to Induce Vomiting in Dogs
by Dawn Ruben, DVM   http://www.petplace.com/
used with permission

Frequently, dogs ingest items, chemicals or foods that have the potential to be dangerous or even toxic to them. If you see this ingestion, you may be able to avoid the potential danger by making your dog vomit.

Inducing vomiting should be done only if instructed by your veterinarian. The procedure can be hazardous. We strongly encourage you to contact your family veterinarian or local veterinary emergency center for advice regarding the appropriateness of inducing vomiting for each specific incident. The item or substance ingested, the time and amount of ingestion, as well as the overall health of your dog should be considered prior to recommending the induction of vomiting.

Methods to Induce Vomiting

Three percent hydrogen peroxide is quite effective in making dogs and cats vomit. You must be sure to use three percent peroxide and not hair coloring strength peroxide.

Despite the label indicating that hydrogen peroxide is toxic, it is safe to give to dogs for this purpose. It is considered toxic since it induces vomiting and therefore does not stay in the body.

The appropriate dose of hydrogen peroxide is one teaspoon per 10 pounds of body weight. If you have an oral syringe, one teaspoon equals 5 cc or 5 ml. Once given, walk your dog around or gently shake the stomach area to mix the peroxide with the stomach contents. Vomiting should occur within 15 to 20 minutes. If no vomiting occurs, you can safely repeat the three percent hydrogen peroxide once. If it is still not effective, your dog may need to be seen by a veterinarian for stronger vomiting medication.

Once the hydrogen peroxide is given, it is important to watch your pet so that he does not re-ingest the substance. If there is concern about toxicity, collect and take a sample of the vomitus to your veterinarian.

Syrup of Ipecac can be dangerous and even toxic to dogs so it should not be used unless specifically advised by your veterinarian.

Charlie's Past Life? - 1/23/10

It's always interesting to conjecture what a rescue dog did in his past life to cause his former owners to finally throw in the towel and take him to the shelter. All we know about Charlie is that he was "given up for being destructive."

Our laptop now has four keys popped off of it. We hold ourselves responsible although Charlie is suspect. While we were snuggled up sleeping, apparently, he was scavenging. I'd left a small bag of kibble on the table where my laptop lives. It seems Charlie did a midnight raid on the table. He wasn't really trying to dismantle the computer. That was just a byproduct of his yummy hunt.

Then there are a few other traits that may have led to his banishment from his former home. For sure, he knew how to escape his yard by "pancaking" himself under the fence. I found him in neighbor Wendy's front yard playing with her dogs a couple of days ago. He feigned deafness when I called him, another trick that has served him well in his past life.

I suspect his reactivity toward other dogs when he's on leash is a result of being used as a "tester" dog while he was in the shelter. He seemed so inoffensive and sweet that the shelter workers used him to test for aggression in other dogs. Now he can quickly become reactive when on a leash and he sees another dog.

Yesterday, he went with me to a training session with a very nice dog who is very reactive toward other dogs when his Mom tries to walk him in town. Her dog is also a rescue. She thought she'd have him trained professionally and sent him away to a trainer who used an e-collar (shock collar) on him. He's never been the same. He now squeals and lunges when he sees a dog in the distance. (See *Why You Don't Want to Use Scary Methods to Train Your Dog,* Chapter 16) We did *walk-bys* for about a half an hour. Charlie was the cool and collected guy. Our work has been paying off.

Gracie

"When Gracie came to me, she had been running wild on a golf course for months. She's become less fearful over time but still didn't warm up to visitors in my home. Even with me, she often didn't want to be petted.

We recently learned the *May I Touch your Body* and *Chin* games. Gracie is acting like a completely different dog! She now approaches me and wants to snuggle and be petted.

Positive clicker training has opened a whole new world in our relationship! Gracie loves it and so do I!"

Mary Jo McLellan

26
THE FINE ART OF LOOSE-LEASH WALKING

Chances are you've already taught your dog how to walk on leash. I'll bet he's already learned that all he has to do is pull and you will follow! Most of us are in such a hurry to take our new dog out in public that we inadvertently teach him to pull when he's on his leash. We let him practice pulling most of the time and then wonder why it takes so much commitment to train him to walk calmly with us without yanking our arm off.

Your dog may pull when on leash for a number of reasons...

❖ Pulling has worked to get him where he wants to go (which is the most likely reason).

❖ He's unable to focus and respond to you because the environment is too stimulating or scary for him to notice you and follow your cues.

❖ His former owners have used painful leash training methods in the past and he associates leash-walking with pain.

Teaching your dog to walk well on leash is all about you training yourself to *only* move ahead with him when he's not pulling on the leash. Your pup has already learned some behaviors that will make it easier to train him to walk nicely on leash.

❖ **Eye Contact** – Have you played the Eye Contact Game with your dog? If so, your dog should be naturally looking at you to get what he wants.

❖ **The Name Game** – You say your dog's name and he looks at you. You can also get him to orient to a sound like a kissy noise.

❖ **Hand Targeting** – The pup will move toward and touch the flat open palm of your hand when you say "touch it."

❖ **Yielding to Pressure** - You've practiced "clicking" and rewarding your dog for moving his body with only light pressure on his harness or collar.

❖ **The Walk Away Game** – Your dog has learned to walk past a cookie on the floor without pulling on his leash. This will help him to focus back on you when there are distractions on his walk.

You can help your dog get into position to walk next to you by leading him using *Hand Targeting*.

Remember that dogs can learn and focus better when they don't have any pressure on their throat. When I am teaching a dog to walk on a leash, I attach the front chest ring of his harness together with the ring of his collar. This makes a secure attachment that allows the dog to naturally reorient toward me if he happens to pull forward. I can then mark and reward him for turning back to me.

Now you can learn and practice a few more games that will all work to make your leash training easier.

Loose Leash Standing – Can your dog stay next to you when he's on a leash and there are distractions nearby? Practice standing in one place and giving him a lot of tiny treats to keep his attention on you. You might practice having a friend walk a dog by at a distance or practice having other family members skipping past.

Find Me Game: This is a great game to help your dog turn his whole body back toward you.

❖ Put a treat on the ground in front of your dog and say "take it." If he's sitting, put the treat far enough in front of him so that he'll have to stand up to move to get the food.

❖ While the dog is eating the treat, quickly step directly behind the dog. When the dog turns his head to look to you for another goodie, say "yes," or "click," and feed him as he turns his whole body toward you.

❖ Immediately put another treat on the ground behind the dog, step behind the dog, and mark and reward him as he turns toward you.

❖ Repeat this sequence a number of times in quick succession until it's hard to step behind the dog because he turns so quickly.

Walking Backwards:

❖ Start with the dog in front of you facing you. Walk backwards a few steps and use hand targeting to get the dog to follow you as you back up. Say "Yes" or "click" the dog as his nose touches your hand.

Now you are ready to practice **moving forward** with your dog.

❖ Walk a few steps backwards, with your dog following your left hand as a target. Then start moving forward and your dog will turn so that both you and your dog are facing the same direction. With your dog on your left side, continue to hand target. Take a few steps forward. Mark the dog's position and movement next to you with a "yes" or "click." Reward him with a treat with your <u>left hand beside your left leg</u>. In other words, give him his treat where you want his body to be.

❖ **Build duration on walking forward.** Whenever the dog moves ahead of you, say his name or make the "kissy" sound to have him reorient to you and start walking backwards a couple of steps, and have him hand target back to you. Then walk forward again once the dog is back next to you. Mark and reward him as he moves along in position next to you.

Practice! Start adding distractions and practicing your new loose-leash walking skill in a variety of environments. Don't expect your dog to be able to immediately walk anywhere you want without pulling. If he starts to pull and become lizard-brained, the environment is too scary or busy for him. He needs to build his confidence in new environments bit by bit. Learn to anticipate distractions such as another dog in the distance or playing children. Be ready to help him stay near you by rewarding him for turning his attention to you instead of lunging on his leash.

If you're in a hurry to get somewhere or you're taking a lazy walk in the woods and you don't want to be consistent about training your dog to walk on a loose leash, sidestep the problem by hooking his leash to the back ring of his harness. That can be his "I don't care if you pull" signal. Then, later when your pup is grown and you want to sled or bicycle with him, he'll know its OK to sometimes pull.

Concert - 2/20/10

Charlie has made his debut in the Howell arts community. Last night we took him to his first concert at the Opera House.

I took along his mat hoping that would be a target where I could intermittently reward him for staying. He had different plans.

He entertained a couple sitting at a table about 10 feet away. He sat and looked cute, he bowed, he smiled, and he stared. He had the couple chuckling and making faces back at him. His goal was to charge over and eat the stray peanuts under their table. I didn't allow that to happen. He spent part of the concert perched on the chair next to us, partly draped across our laps and finally went to sleep half on the chair next to us with his cute little chin resting on my lap.

During breaks he charged people and grabbed their dollars and stuck them in a plastic bowl. He was introduced to the crowd as " Charlie the Money Dog." We are his proud parents!

Charlie practicing "Peanut Agility"
He's becoming obsessed with grabbing peanuts off the floor at the concerts at the Opera House so we're practicing having him work with peanuts as a distraction.

27
THE MAT GAME
FREE SHAPING A BEHAVIOR USING A CLICKER
ADAPTED FROM CHRIS BACH'S **THIRD WAY**™

Does your dog ever get the "zoomies" and have a hard time calming himself down? Wouldn't it be nice to be able to take your dog with you to an outside café and have him quietly rest under your table as you eat? Wouldn't it be nice to take your dog along when you visit relatives and know that he can lie quietly without bouncing around and making himself obnoxious?

This game helps the dog to learn to calm himself by being conditioned to *love* going to his mat and rest there in a "down" position.

If you're training a puppy, you'll first start with a shortcut trick that will help your dog learn the concept of getting his body onto a specific target. You'll reward your pup for getting on a box. (If your dog is already large, you may choose to skip this first section as it's much easier to do with a smaller sized dog, or instead of a box, cut a piece of thick foam insulation to fit his body size.) This may sound like an oblique way to train your dog to go to a mat, but he'll learn the concept of getting his body onto a target more easily if you start with a box first.

You'll need to find a plastic storage box a few inches high that is large enough for your pup to be able to fit his whole body onto it when it's turned upside down. You will use "free shaping" to get the puppy to love being on his box. "Free shaping" means that you won't be placing him on the box or luring him there with food. If you've not tried using a clicker yet, this is a great time for you to hone your clicker training skills. You will be practicing your clicker timing and observational skills while your pup is developing his problem-solving thinking skills.

Remember that "Shaping" a behavior means teaching it incrementally, marking and rewarding all the steps along the way to getting the final behavior you want. You need to start with your final goal in mind and help the pup get to the goal behavior step by step, marking ("clicking") and rewarding each step along the way to your final behavioral goal.

Clicker training is a very powerful training tool. Once you and your dog have mastered the basics, you'll be able to teach many complex behaviors with ease. Dogs learn faster when you use a clicker to train them. The "click" sound is more noticeable to them than saying "yes." Just hearing a "click" will give your dog a surge of joy!

Let's review the basics:

- ❖ **Picture your training goal**. Our first goal will be getting the pup to stand with all four feet on the box.

- ❖ **"Click"** and then reward the second your puppy does a behavior that is a step toward reaching that goal. The timing of your click is most important! Remember, the sound of the "click" is like taking a picture of the behavior. Your "click" needs to happen the exact second the pup is doing the behavior.

- ❖ **You always follow each click with a reward.** Make sure your treats are high value and very small.

- ❖ **Once the pup has completed each training step a couple of times, stop marking and rewarding that step and wait until he offers the next step toward your training goal.** You are "shaping" his behavior toward your goal. If you keep rewarding the same small steps toward your goal, your dog will get "stuck" doing them and not offer new behaviors.

Sit on the floor with your pup in a place away from distractions. Have high value tiny treats ready on a table next to you so you can grab them easily.

- ❖ Set the box down a couple of feet away from your pup. Remember the guidelines for getting the pup used to something new. Review *Introducing New Equipment and Clothes to Your Dog* (Chapter 10). Anytime you're introducing a new object to your dog, assume that he might be frightened of it. "Click" and reward the dog when he looks at the plastic box and then gently pick it up and move it behind you. Repeat this a few times so the dog is wishing you'll bring the box back into view so he'll be rewarded.

- ❖ Place the box about a foot away from your dog and "click" and reward him for looking at it a few times.

- ❖ Now raise your criteria and "click" as he approaches the box. Hand target and reward him for coming away from the box after each approach. It will be important to teach him to come away from the box as well as to approach it.

- ❖ Wait until he approaches the box again and "click" when he touches the box.

At this point, many puppies will just climb onto the box as part of their bouncy puppy behavior. If your pup doesn't climb up, you'll shape the behavior step by step:

- ❖ One foot on the box

- ❖ Two feet on the box

- ❖ Four feet on the box

Once the pup is up on the box, keep him up there by using a quick succession of treats as you learned in the section called *Sit and Sit Some More* (Chapter 17).

Now call him off the box using hand targeting and have him sit. Most pups want to immediately climb back on the box so your job is to have him sit first, and then send him back to the box.

When you're teaching a dog a new trick, you wait to give the trick a name until you're about 90% sure he's going to do the behavior. You don't want to be incessantly saying, "Go to your box," while you're first getting the behavior. By the time he figures out what behavior you're rewarding, your cue word will have become useless babble to him. Always wait to add a cue to a new behavior until the dog is doing the behavior reliably.

Once your pup knows this trick, it may become one of his favorites. You can use it to send him to the scale at the vet's office or target the table if you're doing agility. You can practice sending him from greater distances or increase the amount of time he'll stay on his box.

But what about the mat?

If you've worked on the box trick, teaching your dog to go to a mat will be very easy. Your pup will already know the concept of getting his body onto a target.

You need a small rug, towel or other mat that can be easily picked up and a stash of yummy food rewards.

- ❖ Place the mat on the floor. You can free shape him stepping on the mat as you did with the box. "Click" and reward as you shape his

Darse has graduated from getting on her box to lying on her mat.

behavior toward getting his whole body onto the mat.

❖ Release him, say "go play" and immediately pick up the mat.

❖ Put the mat back down and repeat the procedure.

❖ After couple of trials, he will automatically step onto the mat when you put it down.

❖ Treat him, tell him to "go play" and pick up the mat again.

❖ Repeat this until he is pouncing on the mat when you place it on the floor.

❖ Ask him to "lie down" on the mat and reward him.

❖ Practice placing the mat and having him lie down after his pounce on it.

❖ Now, restrain the dog, put the mat down, have him sit, and now send him to the mat adding a "Go to your mat" cue.

❖ Using his skills from the *Sit and Sit Some More Game,* practice a down-stay with distractions on the mat.

❖ Remember to release the dog from the mat by saying, "Go play."

This is a great trick to take "on the road." First practice the game in all areas of your house, and then, do it outside. Take your dog with you for a cup of tea at a quiet outdoor restaurant. Don't order a full meal yet. You're going to be spending 100% of your time training, not eating. Make sure to reward your dog for remaining on his mat despite distractions: the passing dog, whining kids and folks at the next table ogling over his superb behavior. Gradually increase the time and distraction level your dog can handle.

This trick can become a favorite for both you and your dog. He'll be able to calm himself and stay in one place and you'll enjoy the companionship of having your buddy in many places that dogs usually don't get a chance to go.

Onie

"One of Onie's first tricks as a puppy was to go to her box. She learned the 'Box' command fairly quickly as she received praise and a treat for each successive move toward the box and eventually for sitting on the box. Today at 10 months, we will find Onie proudly showing off, sitting on her box if we leave it out."

Jacquie & Mike Read

Charlie CGC!! - 2/21/2010

Yippee! Hooray! Charlie is now a CGC certified dog!! I took him with me Saturday to do therapy dog testing. I was hoping to bring him out for a few minutes before most of the folks arrived and have him practice walking past other dogs. The first person to arrive for the test was a nice older gentleman who somehow didn't know that a "Leave it" with food was going to be on the test. I grabbed Charlie out of the car and quickly demonstrated how to train his dog. Charlie did better than I expected being near the dog he didn't know. That built my confidence a bit so I took him into the building to use him as the dog to demonstrate the test. I had Kim, the resident trainer run through the test with him. He did great!

She invited him to stay in a crate in the room during the therapy dog testing. I was a bit hesitant about doing that, thinking that he'd probably get bored and start being obnoxious in the crate. He whined just a bit and then settled down. I rewarded him with a few kibbles.

As the testing proceeded, I got brave and grabbed him out of his crate, rather than Reggie, to do the "dog distraction" part of the test. He did it like a pro, except for giving the English Mastiff a cute little "let's go play" nod of his head! I felt a bit guilty when the giant dog broke his position and tried to pull his owner over to Charlie. I retested the big dog later with Reggie and he did just fine.

By the end of the day, I felt confident that he'd pass the whole Canine Good Citizen test including the 3 minute separation. Kim, the trainer who was hosting the therapy dog testing, is a CGC evaluator. She ran Charlie through the testing procedure. He was great and now is an official "Canine Good Citizen!"

28
SIT TO BE PETTED

Think of all the things your dog could be doing when someone tries to pet him:

❖ Jumping on their body

❖ Climbing up their legs

❖ Eating their hands

Wouldn't it be nicer to know that your dog could sit quietly to be petted?

People assume that dogs love to be petted. Although people like to pet dogs, being patted on the head or stroked along the back is not a natural thing for dogs to tolerate or enjoy. In fact, many dogs are uncomfortable with big unfamiliar hands (or little wiggly hands) approaching and touching their bodies. Some dogs just freeze and tolerate the touch but others may become agitated, squirmy or grabby with their mouths as hands move toward their bodies.

Buzz is practicing being calm while being petted.

Our goal is to make being petted a *trick!*

You'll need to already be working on *Sit and Sit Some More* (Chapter 17), your dog is getting good at staying in the sit position when you use distractions, and you have increased the amount of time for him to remain seated.

Do you remember the *May I Touch your Body* game? This will be similar. You'll ask your dog to sit (and wait) and then present your hand. You'll touch the top of his head and then run your hand down his back. Say, "Yes," or "click," reward and then release him to "Go play." Repeat this sequence until he anticipates your hand moving toward him and chooses to remain calm and stationary. Now add the cue, *"pet"* and repeat the stroking a few more times.

Play this game for a few minutes at a time saying the cue "pet" as a cue for him to sit without moving while you run your hand down his body from the top of his head down his back. Release him to "Go Play" after your petting session.

The next step is to vary your petting, a few pats, perhaps a little head tousle, a little body rubbing. Mark and reward his ability to stay seated while doing this trick. Remember, people who meet your dog may have wiggly hands, insist on patting your dog on the head or may have candy goo on their fingers. Add as many variables as you can to this trick. You'd be amazed at the stupid stuff people will do to pet a dog.

Now it's time to generalize this trick with as many people as you can. Start with family members who know the dog well and expand to people of all sizes, ages, colors, weird clothing, cigarette smokers, and anything else you can think of. With small children, you need to be the one who guides their little hands so they don't pull hair or poke.

If your dog is good at picking out cues in sentences, you may start cuing him by saying something like "would you like to **pet** my dog" or "Let me have my dog *sit* so you can **pet** him. Your well-practiced dog's response will be an automatic sit-maintain.

He'll see being petted as a well-rewarded trick rather than scary abuse to be tolerated. You'll be proud of him and he'll see greeting people as a fun, worthwhile activity.

Home Alone & Grounded Center – 3/4/10

Something is changing…. We've hit a different place in our relationship. It's hard to describe. In the last few days Charlie is both less needy yet more in tune with me. I noticed the changes a few days ago. Charlie is becoming a friend and work-mate, yet less needy and more his own person.

I noticed it first while I was working at the computer. He'd come over and try to engage my attention, and look at me as though he was trying to communicate. I'd ask him to do some behaviors and he seemed more intent in his ability to key in on what I was asking for. For a while, he's known the trick of bumping his nose around in a food bowl to express his desire to eat but this was different. He was looking to interact in a more give-and-take way. It's hard to describe but my gut tells me that we're beginning to enter into the relationship that goes beyond me being a cookie machine.

I had some time to kill waiting to rendezvous with some friends while in Ann Arbor a few days ago. I was parked in a nice sunny parking lot well off the road and with no traffic to fear. I took Charlie out of the car and engaged him in some training review. We practiced leash walking, and long distance comes. I brought his mat out and had him practice going to his mat from varying distances. He seemed more centered than I've ever seen him. There weren't any big distractions around, but I didn't fear that he would bolt away. He was "on" and enjoying showing off his skills.

Yesterday, I took him with me to Sydney's house. Syd is a magnificent Ridgeback friend who will soon be getting a sibling puppy. He's a big, exuberant guy who can be overwhelming to other dogs. He's met Charlie before and, at that time, was gentle in his play attempts. Yesterday he had reverted back to wild and crazy attempts to overpower Charlie with rude crotch-sniffing, paw-squishing exuberance. My training goal was to practice calling him from play. In reality, the training session looked more like calling him away from obnoxious dog mauling. The amazing thing in this whole scenario was that Charlie was in total control. A few months ago, I would have had two wrestling dogs – Charlie would have been just as crazy as Syd, diving under his body to grab his legs. Charlie was cool, calm and collected throughout the session.

One of the tough training challenges we've only started to address is Charlie's crazed attitude toward squirrels. We've had a big fat squirrel show up on our deck a few times. Charlie's instant response was to bounce up and down barking at the window. I hoped to nip the behavior in the bud so I grabbed some high value treats and did a quick call away from the window, reward and then sent back to bark. Who would even guess how well this would work to short-circuit the crazed barking. Within a few seconds, Charlie went from a maniac lizard to a responsive Einstein! In fact, the squirrel was still out there munching at bird seed but Charlie was coming to me looking to do more tricks.

Judy, Syd's mom has a whole yard full of bird feeders that attract a constant supply of hungry squirrels. I didn't want to actually let Charlie loose to chase them but instead I cued "get the squirrel" and let him lunge at the end of the leash a bit and then called him back for a reward. He seemed to be catching on to this new game as a way to earn cookies. I look forward to practicing this more. I hope I can mute the crazed lunging and turn this into an operant game.

I've been experimenting with some uncrated "home-alone" time. Up until now, Charlie has always been crated when we're not here. This last week, I was in and out of the house a lot while caring for neighbor Therri's dogs. I was leaving the house for a half to full hour at a time. After a while, I got lazy about crating Charlie and left him loose in the house. It was no big deal. He just hung out on the couches or bed like the other dogs. I'm still not ready to extend the time yet for him to be loose, but this is a beginning.

Now the part that is baffling to me... If Charlie seems so much more grounded and connected, why is he spending more time sleeping off our bed than on? This is OK as having a dog on my pillow was not all that grand... Has his obnoxious and needy behavior been driven by insecurity? Who knows? Maybe I should start rewarding him for hanging out closer but, for now, I'll just see how this plays out.

We had a whole crew of hard-hatted workmen in our yard trimming trees around the electric lines a couple of days ago. Charlie was calm but also not all that interested in them. I'm beginning to guess that a lot of what we all think of as "outgoing, friendly" behavior in dogs is often pre-emptive groveling. The dog is approaching in a lizard brain mode--that is, approaching, jumping, and kissing--to fend off possible aggressive behavior from the unknown newcomer. Something to mull over...

29
THE MAGIC OF TETHERING

No, this section is <u>not</u> about tying your dog outside to his dog house! Tethering is a term used by dog trainers that means connecting your dog to an immovable object so you can help him to learn or practice new behaviors. As mentioned in Chapter 5, *Default Sit for a Crazed, Obnoxious, Lizard-Brained Dog,* sometimes hooking your dog up while you work can speed up your training, especially if your dog has already learned to spend most of his time being an unfocused "lizard brain." Tethering can also help to keep the pup from becoming more engaged with the interesting things in the environment than he is with you.

Working with your dog on a leash is the simplest form of tethering although many seasoned trainers do most of their training by free-shaping their dog off leash. As you become a more practiced trainer you may find yourself using less tethering and doing more of your training with

> *Agility Right from the Start* by Eva Bertilsson and Emelie Johnson Vegh is an outstanding book for learning off-leash handling of your dog

your dog off leash too, but for now, tethering can help you in perfecting some of your dog's skills.

I always use a harness with the leash or tether attached to the back ring. Dogs just don't learn as well when they're stressed by having pressure on their throats.

Some ways to use tethering:

❖ **You can practice having your pup sit when strangers approach him:** (see *Sit to be Petted,* Chapter 28). Hold your dog on a leash. Have a friend approach. Just out of range of your dog, have your friend lead your dog into a lured sit, say "yes," and reward the dog and then walk away. Next have your friend approach close to the dog, but not close enough that he might jump on her. Have her stand there and say <u>nothing</u>. If your dog sits, have her mark and reward him. If your dog starts bouncing, have her turn and walk away.

Repeat these approaches until your dog automatically sits when the friend approaches. Now have her do a bit of petting before she marks and rewards your dog.

❖ **Teach your dog to sit, stand and lie down a distance from you:**
Attach your dog and back up a foot or two away from him. Ask him to "sit." He may look at you quizzically. Dogs learn their tricks contextually, that means, he thinks that part of the sit trick includes you standing right in front of him. When you start changing the context of a trick, the dog can easily become confused. That's why one of your training goals will be to help the dog generalize his tricks to as many different situations as possible.

❖ **Teach your dog to wait or stay:**
When you're playing the *Round Robin Recall* and *Restrained Recall* (Chapter 15) games, your dog will be held before being released to the person who's calling him. Say, "stay" or "wait" as you walk away from him and he'll start to learn those cues.

❖ **Help your dog learn to lie quietly by you while you eat your dinner or work at your computer:**
Connect your dog to your table or chair, give him his mat to lie on and he can learn to take a snooze near you while you're occupied with other things. When he's first learning this trick, make sure you intermittently mark and reward his calm behavior.

Darse is practicing being a calm girl in the living room.

If you're trying to teach your very chewy pup to relax near you, he may decide to eat the leash or your chair rungs while you're engrossed in your meal or work. You may want to put something gross tasting on the furniture so it's not quite so appealing while giving your dog an acceptable chew toy. Your vet and local pet shops have a number of products you can use. You can purchase or make tethers that use plastic-coated steel cable if your dog is a leash shark.

You can order ready-made cable dog tethers at:
http://www.petexpertise.com

Caution: Never make the mistake I made many years ago with my dog Kaddi. I was working at Dog Scout Camp teaching a class. I had Kaddi tethered to my chair. I got up to explain something to a camper and bumped the chair a bit as I arose. Kaddi jumped aside and then took off panicked around the room with the "evil" chair chasing her. To this day, ten years later, she still quivers in fear at the sound of folding chairs and still balks every time I take her into the scary camp lodge where the "evil attack chairs" live.

Science Teachers' Convention, Cobo Dog Show – 3/11/10

This week it was so nice to be at a venue where the Darwin name makes sense – a convention of science teachers! Dear Charlie had a very busy week - a coyote program at the library, two days of science teachers' convention and a day at the giant Detroit dog show.

We spent the science teachers' convention attempting to hide from the two service dog puppies that were in attendance. I met with one of the puppy Moms early the first morning and practiced walk-bys with Lacey and Charlie. Lacey seems to have regressed. We'd just about complete a pass and she'd still slip out a quick little bark. The last thing in the world I need is for Charlie to learn Lacey's dog reactivity.

I decided to shield him from this crazy behavior as much as I could by stuffing Lacey back in the car and walking Charlie through the convention hall with either Reggie or Kaddi. Charlie had never been in such a big noisy space before but handled it without missing a beat. I was brave and left the belly band at home. The random peeing has abated. I was careful, however to schedule lots of potty breaks throughout the day. Despite all the care I had taken to not let it happen, he lunged and barked at the service dog puppy a couple of times. He was a total lizard brain for a few seconds, before turning back to me and sitting. He also managed to escape the presentation room a couple of times to run out and schmooze with teachers passing by in the hall. It was cute, but not my preferred behavior.

Charlie was attentive during the dog program and even rode Anja's scooter! The crowd loved him. He kept sticking his nose in the doggie basketball hoop trying to win a treat. When teaching a complex trick, I teach the last part of the behavior first. Now, it's probably time to teach him the rest of the trick.

We decided to take Charlie and Reggie to the big dog show and leave more reactive Lacey at home. Bob still was slightly out of sorts from having a cold. There was no sense making undue trouble for ourselves.

Charlie pooped three times during the day. He must have had a back-log of goodies in his system from three days of training and doing tricks! Luckily, all the poops were outside, two on the sidewalk in the big city. (Yes, of course we picked them up.) The traffic, noises and big buildings didn't seem to bother him at all. He wisely did not lunge or bark at the hundreds of show dogs and maintained his composure.

I ended up doing three training demonstrations for a few hundred people at the show. Charlie was amazing!! He did his heeling, targeting, retrieves and recalls flawlessly in the big ring in front of lots of people in the bleachers. I'm so used to having scared, socially sensitive dogs. Charlie was able to perform in a completely strange, noisy environment.

Yesterday, I took him with me to dog train in Ann Arbor. After doing tons of walk-bys with the resident dog, Ralph, we demonstrated going to his mat and jumping tricks on the sidewalk and in the cul-de-sac where Bonnie, Ralph's mom lives. I was watchful for squirrels and other distractions that might inspire him to charge off and so I only had him loose off his leash for a few minutes. No sense testing fate before I've taught him to come away from squirrels.

Charlie debuts as a presenter at the Michigan Science Teachers Association conference.

30
THE GLORIES OF USING A LONG LINE

A 30' cotton long line can be a wonderful training tool. It's far safer to use than a retractable leash. If you've ever used one, you know it's pretty easy for them to get yanked right out of your hand. They pose another problem because, no matter how far your dog ranges from you, there's always tension on the retractable line. It's much harder to teach your dog to walk on a loose leash if he's used to feeling tension on his collar all the time.

Many people assume that their dog will just learn to come, no matter what the distractions might be. They'll think the dog is being stubborn, or "blowing them off," if he doesn't respond to their calls, rather than realizing that they just need to do more training. A long line is a wonderful way to let your dog range some distance from you without worrying that he might be too distracted to come when you call him. If need be, you can always gently reel him in and guide him back to you.

With your dog on a long line, you can teach him a wonderful cue, the word "stop." The word "stop" means just that, the dog will stop his forward movement. Then you can either call him to you, or do a sit or down at a distance.

The "stop" cue is very easy to teach if your dog is on a long line. All you need to do is say "stop" every time he reaches the end of the line. Being a positive trainer, you don't want to jerk him to a stop. Use either the back or chest ring attachment of his harness so there's no possibility of accidently bringing him to an abrupt stop and hurting his neck.

You may find it works best to let the line drag on the ground and then step on it to limit your dog's distance from you. When you step on the line, make sure you increase your foot's pressure on the line gradually so the dog won't be jerked to a stop. Let some of the line slide a bit under your foot as you are stepping down on it.

Look What I Found!

German dog trainer, Clarissa von Reinhardt, suggests a wonderful game to play with your dog while on relaxed walks on a long line. Your dog's natural tendency will be to explore the environment. He'll be sniffing the air and nosing the ground. What if magical things to explore just happened to be where you helped to point them out to your dog? What if *you* could be the one who was best at finding surprise goodies along the way?

Clarissa suggests that you "plant" special treats among the bushes and brush as you walk. Bend over and point to the ground and say, "Look what I found!" You may have to call your dog over to you the first few times so he'll get close enough to find the treat that you've hidden. Pretty soon, your dog will keep a close eye on you as you hike with him. He'll watch your body language to see if you're finding interesting things along the way. He'll spend more time near you and focused on you than on other smells and distractions.

Order Clarissa von Reinhardt's excellent book, *Chase! Managing Your Dog's Predatory Behavior* at www.DogWise.com

Enjoy your walks with your dog!

Charlie is looking for treats hidden along the road rather than searching for bunnies!

The Sneak - 4/7/10

Just about now, I'm wishing I had adopted a pristine puppy that I could have trained rather than a "used" rescue who came with problems. I would never have allowed this to happen if I were his mom from the start.

It started with the great escape at Granny's house. I was busy poop-picking in her back yard when, all of a sudden, Charlie was chasing squirrels in the neighbor's yard. By the time I got through the garage and out of her fenced yard, he was peeing on a tree across the street.

The bad news is that Charlie thinks nothing about getting out of a fenced yard to romp the neighborhood. The good news is that he didn't get squished on the road or attacked by a neighbor's dog. Also it was good that he happily approached me after a long minute of feigning deafness before responding to my calls.

Back at home the next day, his wanderlust had become compulsive. He became hell-bent on leaving. It seemed every time I looked away for a second, he was purposefully trotting out toward the front gate, and if I didn't call him away immediately, he'd start pushing the bungee secured gate with his paw. We were working in the yard, and, all of a sudden, Charlie was gone. As Bob dashed toward the front gate, I spied the tip of a white tail above the dried weeds in the field next door. I hopped the fence and encountered the little imp nosing through the brush. He seemed conflicted about coming back to the yard with me. At first, he trotted a couple hundred feet away. He finally responded to my "stop" and "sit" cues. "Come" didn't work at all.

Back in the yard, I realized that one of my new garden gloves had vanished. I showed Charlie the other one and tried a "go find it" cue. It would have been nice if that worked, but I really hadn't practiced that game very much, so Charlie just stared at me blankly.

I tried a different tactic. I tossed the remaining glove on the ground. Charlie snatched it up and merrily trotted away to the edge of the woods where he dug a hole and buried it!! This did not bode well for ever finding the other glove. He could have stashed it just about anywhere.

I scratched around the area where he'd just buried my remaining glove. I called him over and said "find it." He dug around in the leaves and proudly pulled up the glove. I became ecstatic with praise and charged to the house with him for a cookie party. He got a whole tuna cookie for his splendid work, a lot more than he ever gets at one time. Then I tucked another whole cookie in my pocket showed him the just-found glove and told him he'd get the big cookie if he could find the other glove that he had stolen earlier. Wouldn't you know it, a half hour later, the lost glove magically appeared!

Now my training tasks:

- ❖ Fortify the fencing at my mom's house – put chicken wire across the gate opening and across the gap where the fence connects to the house

- ❖ Never assume that Charlie is safe in a fenced enclosure

- ❖ Be more mindful of where Charlie is when I'm in the yard with him

- ❖ Tether Charlie near where I'm working in the yard when I'm not actively watching or interacting with him.

- ❖ Practice zillions of recalls, distance stop, sits and downs with lots of rewards

- ❖ Practice the *Bad Dog Retrieve* outside. I had made a big mistake. I had only practiced the game inside the house. He's so great at this inside, why didn't I think to be more mindful about practicing this trick outside?

- ❖ Start playing tracking and finding games outside

The glove

31
KEEPING TRACK OF YOUR PROGRESS

If you've been systematically working through this book, your dog should be developing a good vocabulary. You've been teaching him new cues and hopefully clarifying others that you may have already been using.

The key to having your dog understand your cues is to be as consistent as possible. If you give a cue and he doesn't respond, then you need to back up and look at your training history with that cue.

- ❖ Maybe you assumed he knew a behavior that you never really taught and practiced. Often people assume their dog will "come" just because they "said so!"

- ❖ Maybe your dog has been relying on the context of the cue, for example, if you teach him to sit in the kitchen in front of the refrigerator, he may not understand that he can do the same behavior in the living room.

- ❖ Your dog may not be learning verbal cues well because you've always paired them with body motions and he's been responding to them, rather than your spoken words. (see *Sits, Downs & Stands,* Chapter 17)

- ❖ The environment may be too distracting for the dog to do the behavior or the dog is afraid of something. When I was at camp in Vermont with my dog Anja, all-of-a-sudden, she "forgot" how to retrieve. She started sniffing the ground instead of bringing back the metal spoon I had thrown. I couldn't figure out what had come over her. (Ground sniffing is often a sign of stress, by the way.) It turned out that the instructor's dog was glaring at her, resource guarding the spoon, from about 10 feet away where the dog was reclining in a chair!

Remember how long it took you to learn Algebra? You started simply, learned the basic skills, practiced them and then used them in tougher and tougher problems. You'll want to help your dog learn his training skills in the same way.

The most effective way for you to access your dog's progress is to keep some sort of training journal. Just as we did with the *May I Touch Your Body Game* and the *Sensitivity Assessment Chart* (Chapter 12). You'll want to date your entry and watch your progress over time.

For each behavior you put on cue for your dog, you'll want to see how advanced you can get with that particular trick. For example if your dog can sit and wait on cue, can he do that trick while you bounce a ball near him. Can he "sit" if you ask him to do so from 20 feet away? How long can he sit?

You'll be amazed at how skilled your dog can become!

Training Record

Date:_____ Basic Behaviors	Preliminary Shaping	Behavior Perfected	Put on Cue	Performance with Distractions	Performance at Distance	Duration
Sit						
Stay						
Come						
Stand						
Down						
Bring it here						
Get it						
Pick it up/Take it						
Drop it						
Leave it						
Touch it						
Go						
Hold it						
Heel						
Catch it						
Stop						
Jump up on						
Wait/Stay						

Charles Unleashed! - 6/19/10

We're just back from Charlie's first week at Dog Scout Camp. I'm still in disbelief. The funny little dog who entered our lives last fall may be evolving into a pretty neat little guy after all. A week before camp, I would have never guessed how well he'd do.

He cleaned up on earning badges. Before camp, he'd already qualified for his Dog Scout certification, retrieve and painting badges so we arrived primed for more.

He skimmed through his agility obstacle badges. Our bit of jumping, teeter and tunnel training at home prepped him for success. Our friend and mentor Jill coached us on some new weave pole training. By the end of the week, Charles pretty much had that figured out.

Our heeling and "Leave it" practice helped us navigate the Rally course.

I wasn't sure Charles would ever make it past the "panty line" swimming, only getting himself wet up to his tummy, until camper Linda loaned us a chunk of frozen venison to encourage him to brave deeper water. He's like a little bobbing cork in the water. I think he could stay afloat without paddling at all. Once he got the swimming part tackled, he easily skimmed through his boating and "beach buddy" requirements.

Badges aside, the Charles I saw at camp is a guy who is finally becoming my buddy not just a cookie monger. He did escape from the fenced enclosure behind the staff cabin so many times it became a game. He just doesn't see fencing as a barrier. The good news is he didn't run off after his escapes. At one point, he wriggled through the fence in a mad dash after Lonnie's cat. I tore around the front of the cabin hoping to find him and hopefully a still-live kitty. I found the two of them sitting on the front porch of the trailer. The very wise cat had quickly educated him about the power of spitting and claws. The game was over and the two of them were at peace.

I never thought I'd trust Charles for a second off leash, but I found myself comfortable having him loose for short jaunts within camp. Our morning walks were safely on leash or dragging a long line

I guess I was most surprised by Charlie's calm behavior during lectures in the building and his relaxed attitude toward all the other dogs at camp. I've taken him to a few meetings with me and have practiced his staying power on a mat but I never expected him to be so good at this trick.

Now it's time to plan for our next camp....which badges will we work on next!?

Charlie loved learning agility at camp!

One of the requirements for Charlie's Dog Scout "Beach Buddy" badge is to be able to do a "leave-it" on the beach. He's walking past a lasagna pan!

32
TRAINING CHALLENGES

"How do I stop my dog from jumping on people? My dog is barking in his crate. My dog is hiding from little kids. My dog is driving me crazy!" Dog trainers hear those complaints all the time. It seems that people want a one-line answer to solving their dog's behavioral problems. Maybe you've heard of training techniques that involved scaring the dog in some way to change his behavior, like the old idea of kneeing a dog in the chest to teach him to stop jumping on people. Or you've been watching too many TV dog training shows where they solve all the training problems in a half hour.

When you are working to change a behavior that you don't like, you're going to need a training plan. Just scaring your dog or saying, "No," may temporarily suppress a behavior but that's not going to help your dog know what to do instead.

For your training plan, you'll need to consider these elements:

❖ What is the behavior you want to change?

You will need to be specific. Just saying, "The dog barks too much." is way too general. Maybe he's barking at a passersby or, maybe, he's barking to get tidbits from the table while you're eating. In most cases, you'll be working on one specific behavior at a time.

❖ What triggers this behavior?

If he's barking for scraps from the dinner table, the problem could be the presence of Grandma who likes to slip him goodies. If he's jumping on people at the door it could be his level of excitement at meeting people he doesn't know.

❖ How is the dog currently being rewarded for continuing to do the behavior you don't like?

Dogs do what works best for them. They experiment with different behaviors just like any other thinking animal. The behaviors that work to help them get what they want will become more common. So, in the example of barking at the table, someone must have rewarded the dog with a tidbit from the table. Perhaps the dog begged and looked cute, so Grandma sneaked a food morsel to him.

Getting a reward occasionally is a *very* strong motivator. Have you ever thought about how crazy it is to put a quarter in a slot machine? People stand in front of the machines for hours, giving the casino their hard earned cash, just because they *very* occasionally get some of it back. Our pet dogs are a lot like those crazed gamblers. If a behavior gives them a reward every once in a while, they'll keep playing the odds and repeat the behavior.

❖ Is everyone in the family committed to changing the behavior?

You've got to be fair to your dog. If you don't want him doing an obnoxious behavior, everyone who regularly interacts with the dog must agree to the training program that will change his behavior. Inconsistency leads to "testing" behavior. The dog is continually trying to figure out what works best with each person he encounters. His behavior will seem inconsistent. If some members of the family pet him when he jumps all over their bodies, he will continue to do the jumping despite other family members working to train another behavior.

You may want to make a simple chart to deal with your training challenges:

Dog's behavior that we want to change	How is the dog currently being rewarded for this behavior?	What factors are triggering this behavior?
Dog barking at table during meals	Grandma occasionally feeds him	Presence of Grandma Presence of food
Dog jumping on people	Some people pet him when he's climbing on their bodies	New people at the front door

Once you've defined the problem you can start working on a plan to modify behaviors you don't want your dog to practice. Often people react to a behavior they don't like by yelling, "No!" at their dogs. That's not going to get you results over the long haul. You're just temporarily suppressing the behavior. The problem with using suppression to attempt to stop your dog from doing something is that it doesn't give your dog a chance to be rewarded for an alternate behavior. Training means increasing the probability that your dog will do behaviors you like, not just shutting the dog down by yelling at him.

Often, what happens in a household where someone (frequently it's the guy in the family) tries to change the dog's behavior through scare tactics, the dog will seem to be good with the suppressor but will be a total maniac lizard with the less forceful members of the family. A dog who is being bullied in this way often will pick on other members of the family or be totally unmanageable for them. You want to change your dog's behavior through positive training methods, not scare tactics.

Your plan for changing your dog's behavior needs to be based on considering a number of factors:

- ❖ How can you manage the triggers that precede the behavior?

  In the case of Grandma feeding the dog from the table, you might just stop inviting her over for dinner, although that might be a bit extreme. It might be better to manage her by explaining your new training program and rewarding her for alternate behavior!

- ❖ What alternate behaviors can you reward that will replace the undesired behavior?

  You could reward your dog for lying quietly on his mat during meals by giving him a stuffed Kong™ toy to enjoy while you're eating.

- ❖ Are there health concerns that need to be dealt with to reduce the occurrence of the behavior?

  When dealing with house soiling issues, you'll want to work with your veterinarian to make sure that your dog is not dealing with internal parasites or a urinary tract infection. Thyroid problems can make your dog edgy and increase your dog's level of aggression.

- ❖ How can you prevent the behavior from being rehearsed while you're working on your training program?

  While you're working on your retraining project, you'll want to make sure that your dog has no chance to rehearse the behavior you're trying to eliminate. If your dog jumps all over visitors at the front door, and you don't have time to monitor and reinforce an alternate behavior, you'll want to contain him elsewhere in the house when guests arrive.

For each training challenge you tackle, you'll be using a number of tactics to change the unwanted behavior that your dog has been practicing. The easiest way to visualize your training program will be to use a simple diagram. You'll start by making a circle in the center of a page. In the circle, you'll define your training challenge. Next, you'll brainstorm all the tactics that you're going to use to reshape your dog's behavior. Make sure you include:

- ❖ Health issues that need to be checked by your vet

- ❖ Triggers to the behavior that you could prevent from happening

- ❖ Management measures that you'll need to implement to keep the behavior from happening while you're working on your training program

- ❖ Behaviors that you can reward and increase that are incompatible with the obnoxious behaviors you are trying to extinguish

You'll be amazed! If you spend a short time filling out one of these work sheets, you'll be much more organized about helping your dog learn behaviors that are acceptable to your family. You'll be working with your dog rather than just trying to control him.

Here are a few examples of what your charts might look like:

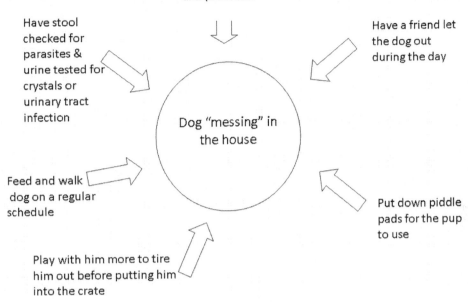

Feed the dog high quality food with pre and probiotics

Have stool checked for parasites & urine tested for crystals or urinary tract infection

Have a friend let the dog out during the day

Dog "messing" in the house

Feed and walk dog on a regular schedule

Put down piddle pads for the pup to use

Play with him more to tire him out before putting him into the crate

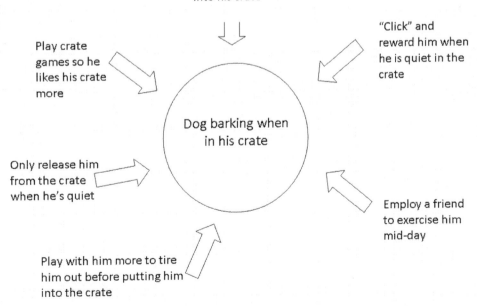

Give him a stuffed Kong™ when he goes into his crate

Play crate games so he likes his crate more

"Click" and reward him when he is quiet in the crate

Dog barking when in his crate

Only release him from the crate when he's quiet

Employ a friend to exercise him mid-day

Play with him more to tire him out before putting him into the crate

Training Challenge Worksheet

Dog's behavior that we want to change	How is the dog currently being rewarded for this behavior?	What factors are triggering this behavior?

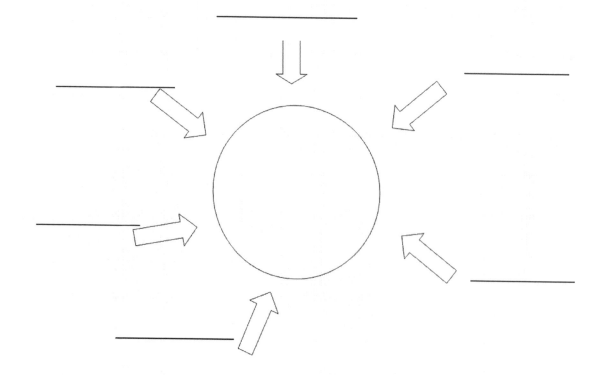

Aggression Training Challenges

Aggression is a normal part of being a dog. A dog can bark, growl, or snap to defend his possessions, protect himself when he is scared, or chase, grab and kill as his canine ancestry has genetically programmed him to do. Unfortunately, his natural behaviors can get him into life-threatening trouble when used in contexts that are unacceptable to humans. None of us can afford the liability of owning a dog that kills the wrong things or bites kids to defend himself.

Why this Dog? Why Me?

Your dog's aggression most likely has both a genetic and a learned component. In most cases, who he is physiologically contributes to his propensity to act aggressively. If his aggression is predatory, he is chasing and biting; he may be from a breed that has been selected to herd sheep or to kill vermin. Unfortunately, he is chasing something or somebody you do not want him to chase. If he is acting defensively, he may be protecting himself because of an edgy personality or because he has learned to protect himself because of scary experiences.

Kaddi's brother Dowda lives with our daughter Kate. Can you tell he was feeling very threatened when this picture was taken?

Some important facts about dog aggression

❖ Prevention is easier than trying to change your dog once he's learned that aggression works for him. Empathize with your dog and watch for signs of stress and distress. Remove him from environments that are more than he can handle.

> *Click to Calm - Positive Answers for the Aggressive Dog* is a wonderful book by trainer Emma Parsons.

❖ Without careful intervention and training, aggression is likely to get worse, not better. Once aggression "works" for the dog, he is more likely to become more aggressive.

❖ Aggression in itself can become rewarding to the dog.

❖ Health issues and chemical imbalances can contribute to aggression in dogs.

❖ Punitive training methods to stop aggression are more likely to make it worse. They may appear to work because they suppress behavior, but the aggression will resurface to haunt you. Overall, the dog will become more reactive and defensive.

- ❖ Aggressive dogs can learn more socially acceptable behaviors, but it is going to take lots of careful hard work to teach the dog new ways of responding.

- ❖ Never assume your dog is "cured" of his aggressive behavior. You will need to spend his lifetime managing him - preventing him from rehearsing aggression, by managing his environment, and helping him to act in socially acceptable ways.

- ❖ Sadly, sometimes an aggressive dog's behavior cannot be changed enough for the dog to continue to live with you. Most likely, you will not be able to find anyone else who wants a dog with his behavior problems and you will need to make the tough decision to have the dog humanely euthanized.

The road to a safer dog…

- ❖ Have the dog thoroughly vet checked for any health problems that may be contributing to his aggression.

- ❖ Seek professional help from a positive dog trainer

- ❖ Learn the exact triggers that precede his aggressive episodes.

- ❖ Watch for the triggers. Learn to intervene **before** the aggression starts.

- ❖ Teach the dog new behaviors to use in aggression-inducing situations.

Dowda is really a very gentle sensitive guy. Kate has learned to manage his environment so he's not placed into scary situations that he can't handle.

- ❖ Manage the dog's behavior and environment to stop aggression before it starts.

Victoria and Beth

If you are dealing with aggression issues, you will want to consult with a positive trainer to help you devise a training plan. Popular TV Trainer, Victoria Stilwell, maintains a listing of trainers who will use positive methods to work with your dog. Find that list at: www.positively.com

Concert in the Park – 7/2/10

We've been preparing for months for last night's big event – the first concert in the park. For the last few years, our dear Anja dog had become a main fundraiser for our arts council by begging for donations at the summer outdoor concerts. Picture hundreds of people in lawn chairs or on blankets on the ground, lots of bubbly children scampering about, open pizza boxes, ice cream cones and cuddly pups in old ladies' laps. Anja was a master of ignoring all these distractions and walking up to people and grabbing their dollar donations and stuffing them in a bucket.

Last evening, dear Charles made his debut as the new donation dog.

We've been preparing for months. He's perfected his panhandling skills during the Christmas season, as a volunteer bell-ringer for the Salvation Army. Our friends at the arts council welcomed Charles as a special guest for the indoor concert season at the Opera House so he'd had a chance to be near blaring speakers and pounding drums. He's perfected his "sit to be petted" trick. The dogs in laps and pizza boxes were to be our biggest challenge.

He was wonderful! After a few moments of bouncing and attempted yapping at the first dog he saw, he calmed himself and settled into the nice relaxed inter-dog behavior he had at camp. He was able to work despite all the food in people's hands. The food on the ground was our biggest challenge. As the evening progressed, popcorn and used pizza paper plates and boxes collected around the lawn chairs and on the corners of blankets. It was like a "leave it" obstacle course!! He did manage to grab one abandoned pizza crust which I quickly extricated from his cute little mouth. He sat to be petted while kids scampered around him.

Charlie "The Money Dog"

Charlie is now a major supporter of The Livingston Arts Council (http://www.theoperahouse.us/). He circulates through the audience at the summer concerts and collects donations. All the folks at the concerts love to give their money to Charlie!

Baloo and Maddy

Baloo

"We have learned so much with positive training techniques, we are all now a little less stressed! Baloo is now capable of so many 'tricks' and behaviors that now we can combine what we've learned and continue growing. However, for us the most basic fundamental behavior is the 'default.' At any time when we approach Baloo or Baloo approaches us he immediately positions himself directly in front of the person and sits. Once sitting, he knows that nothing more will happen until he makes eye contact, which now occurs instantaneously. That loyalty and respect works both ways and is truly a blessing."

The Ayers Family

33
ENTERTAINING YOUR DOG

"And how do you plan to entertain your dog?" That seems like a silly query but I've remembered that wise question scientist Dr. Ray Coppinger asked at a seminar I attended many years ago. Ray has done a lot of work studying dogs and theorizing about how dogs and humans came to share their lives together. All of us who've worked with captive wolves know that our ancestors didn't raise wolf puppies and turn them into pets. Even when they're socialized with people, wolves are too intense, destructive, and unrestrainable to be enjoyed like domestic dogs. Ray's theory is that dogs domesticated themselves. Some of the smaller Mid-Eastern wolves (DNA studies tell us those are the major progenitors of our dogs), started hanging around human settlements eating garbage. The least fearful ones survived and became the ancestors of the dogs we know today.

The fact remains, however, all the dog behaviors that can drive you crazy -- dissecting your best shoes, barking at your friends, wanting to kill the neighbor's dog and peeing on your new couch - come from behaviors that have survival benefits to the wolf ancestors of your dog. Likewise, all the traits that you love about your dog come from his wolf heritage -- his devotion to you, his willingness to bark at strangers, the fun he has chasing his Frisbee™, and his love of exploring with you when you go for hikes. The problem is, your dog has all those behaviors and he's going to use them somehow. If you don't channel his energy into activities that you can tolerate or enjoy, he's likely to invent outlets that will make you wonder why you ever chose to get a dog!

Your job is going to be to find some activities that will best "entertain" your dog. The games that your dog likes best are going to be somewhat related to his breed background. If his working ancestors were herders, expect a dog who can become addicted to chasing. If his parentage includes hunting dogs, expect him to want to use his nose, or if of retriever lineage, expect him to be obsessed with pursuits that involve running around with a toy stuck in his mouth.

You'll be looking for activities that you can enjoy together that make use of his natural behaviors but channel his energy into pursuits that are socially acceptable for a dog living in a human society. It might not be legal for him to run miles off-leash through your neighborhood, but teaching him to pull a sled in winter or bike with you in the summer will give him a similar thrill and lots of exercise. Don't be limited by his breed type, in fact, you may have a border collie who learns to love dog sledding or a beagle who loves water retrieving. Just explore as many possibilities as you can. You'll be surprised at how talented your dog can become and how much fun you'll have doing things together.

The Need to "Seek"

How many people do you know who will spend hours in a freezing trout stream, just so they can let the fish go after they've caught it, or people who "shop 'till they drop" even though they already have a closetful of clothes? Scientists are now realizing that animals have a need to "seek." In other

Find out more about emotions of animals especially the drive to "seek" in Temple Grandin's book, *Animals Make us Human*

words, it's not the end result that's often our goal, but getting there is what gives us pleasure.

Temple Grandin, an autistic scientist and researcher, has given us new insights into the importance of enriching the lives of both farm animals and our pets. Pigs need to have a chance to use their "rooting" behavior to remain sane on farms. Chickens need to be able to walk around and scratch and peck at the ground.

Our pet dogs also need to fulfill their innate seeking behavior. It's not so much holding the ball in his mouth, but the process of running after it that causes your dog to want to retrieve over and over again. When we use positive training methods with our dogs, they're not just wanting to get a treat, but they gain pleasure from the act of working for it.

Some of the best entertainment you can find for your dog will make use of his "seeking" drive. Dogs love to find things, especially by using their noses. Here are three simple activities that can use up some of your dog's energy:

❖ Go find the kibble – Dogs *love* to sniff and find things with their noses. Instead of having your dog follow his nose to dig up moles or chase bunnies, why not toss a handful of his kibble out into your yard for him to find?

Dogs searching for kibble in the snow Notice that they're very busy and not thinking about running off even though the gate is wide open.

❖ Go find your toy – You can play this a lot like the restrained recall game. You have your dog "wait" (tether him if necessary) while you hide his toy and then send him to find it. You can play this inside and out and get as complex as you want. Your dog will become an expert at following your scent trail to his hidden toy.

There's a sport called Canine Nose Work." You can take classes and even compete against other dogs. Find out more at: http://www.k9nosework.com/

❖ Treasure boxes – Have your dog "wait." Put a goodie in one of a number of cardboard boxes you set out. Your dog will learn to look in all the boxes to find the treat. For more of a challenge, use more boxes and spread them out over a larger area. Dogs love this game!

The Duman dogs wait to be sent to their treasure boxes.
This is a great way to practice having your dogs wait despite distractions.

The dogs take off in a mad scramble to get to the boxes. Small treats have been hidden inside some of the boxes.

The dogs are busily searching for the hidden goodies. The boxes have been put close together for this photo, but usually they'd be spread out over a much larger area.

Lots of Entertainment Ideas

I've been a core staff trainer for Dog Scouts of America for many years. Lonnie Olson, Dog Scout's founder, had a dream to have a camp training experience that was open to all breeds and ages of dogs. There would be no limitations on which type of dog could participate in which activity. We started out awarding dogs for the more common dog activities like agility and flyball. As our dogs earned more badges, we kept inventing new ones. As of this writing, we have over 75 activities that our dogs can learn! The Dog Scout web site gives specific training ideas for the badges and can give you an idea of the many fun things you can do with your dog.

Check out the "badges" section at *www.DogScouts.org*
You'll find lots of ideas for fun things to do with your dog and good training information to help you teach him new skills

Oliver

"Oliver mastered the first concept of hand targeting via clicker training immediately with Beth's expertise. After learning all of the basic commands with positive training, Beth moved on to more advanced tricks, from jumping through hula-hoops to dancing on two legs. Then it was time to go outside and start distance learning. One of the concepts mastered was distance tethering. The 'trick' was to let Oliver run ahead of us on a 30 foot lead and give the verbal command of STOP! He freezes in his tracks and waits patiently for us to call him back. On command, he comes to us and sits. We vary the distance he gets ahead of us before giving the command and duration that he waits before calling him back. This concept is so important for a dog's safety.

Beth is wonderful. Oliver absolutely can't wait to see which new and creative tricks Beth will bring on her visits. She is gentle and only uses positive reinforcement. Because of her guidance, Oliver has matured from a timid, abandoned shelter dog to passing his Canine Good Citizen test. Oliver is in training to become a certified therapy dog. Beth put a wag in Oliver's tail, now we want Oliver to put smiles on the faces of those in hospitals and elder care facilities."

Lenore Hiscoe and Bob Starr

One Year Anniversary! – 10/1/10

Remember the school where Charles peed all over me the day after I got him last year? We've now marked our 1 year anniversary with this silly little dog by returning to that school this week.

Charles and I have both come a long way since then. Not wanting to repeat the peeing incident, I've become much more proactive in making sure he gets out for regular bathroom breaks. I think that will always be an issue for him so I'll just need to keep on top of the situation.

Comparing him to last year at this time:

- ❖ He now knows many behaviors: sit, down, stay, heel, relax, come, wait, etc...

- ❖ He can calm himself – relax on a mat or without one and stay in one place

- ❖ He can walk past kids to be petted without climbing on their bodies

- ❖ I was able to send him outside for a break with students and he was relaxed

- ❖ I trusted him to follow me to the car without holding the end of his leash

We trained some new behaviors during the course of the day. We had him doing recalls running past food and taught him how to toss litter in the recycle bin. He rode Anja's scooter like a pro.

I noticed something new in Charlie today. After a year of doing tricks and being a cookie monger, I started to see him looking to me more as a working partner. It's hard to explain but I think we are finally becoming a team!

Remember the glove that Charlie stole last summer? That's now his favorite "go find" object. He has to wait while I hide it in the brush, wait until I return to send him for it, and then bring it back. He'll play this game forever and never gets bored.

Winnie

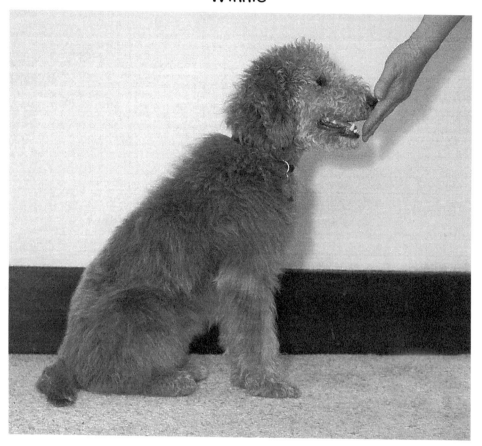

"We knew that Winnie was smart, but it had been 20 years since our last puppy, and our old training methods weren't working. Within a day of starting to use Beth's methods, we had Winnie walking nicely on a leash instead of doing her impression of a 15-pound sled dog, and we could lead her through the house by playing 'Touch.' The training is fun for Winnie, which makes it fun for us. In just a week, we've seen remarkable changes in her behavior. She's the puppy we wanted her to be, and we're the owners she deserves.

Beth has given us the tools to 'reboot' our relationship with Winnie. It is really important to us that Winnie develops the manners that will make her a pleasure at home and anywhere dogs are welcome in the community. We know now that we can accomplish that."

Diana Kohler and Ralph Bruechert

34
TO TUG OR NOT TO TUG

I met a very nice dog yesterday. Millie is a rescue who is looking for someone who has the time and focus to teach her some new rules for playing tug. She's not going to be able to stay at her new adoptive home because her zeal to "play" is dangerous to the two small kids in her family. She's grabbing and pulling anything, whether it's attached to a human body or not. She's already bruised her mom's arm and tried to drag one of the kids across the backyard by his sweatshirt. Millie's behavior is the result of tug training gone wrong!

Millie is a tug maniac - a game gone wild!

Tug can be a wonderful game for your dog if it's played according to rules that keep the game safe. When a dog becomes addicted to playing without rules, the dog can become grabby, jumpy and unsafe with small people. You'll need to decide if tug will be a safe game to play with your dog. If you have family members who might not follow the guidelines for playing tug safely, you may want to suggest that the dog not be introduced to the tug game at all.

The guidelines for playing tug need to be very clear to both your dog and the humans with whom he interacts:

- ❖ Tug games are only instigated by people, not the dog.

- ❖ Tug is only played with articles that are chosen by humans not the dog

To play the game of tug:

- ❖ Offer the tug toy saying, "take it," and then, "pull." If the dog is not immediately interested, try enticing him to get it by dragging the toy back and forth in front of him or offering it to him and quickly pulling it away.

- ❖ After about five seconds of pulling, stop tugging and slip a small tidbit of food into his mouth behind the toy. He'll release the toy as he notices the food in his mouth.

- ❖ Immediately reward him with another piece of food and ask him to sit.

- ❖ Once he's sitting, present the toy, have him tug again for a few seconds and repeat the previous steps to have him release the toy and sit.

- ❖ Add a cue word for the release, like ,"let go," or "out" and continue to practice the sequence of sitting, tugging, release and sitting again.

Keep the game low key until he knows this sequence well. If he gets too rowdy, have him sit and calm himself before resuming play.

Again, only teach the tug game if you are going to practice starting and stopping the game on cue. If you suspect your family or visitors to your home might not follow the tug "rules," please don't teach this game to your dog.

Lacey has learned the rules for playing tug safely.

35
TRAINING ADVANCED BEHAVIORS

If you've been working through the training information in this book, your dog will have learned some basic behaviors that you can now put together to teach more advanced behavior chains that will wow your friends.

What looks like a simple trick can actually be a combination of many trained behaviors strung together. For example, let's look at the trick of having your dog retrieve a dumbbell over a jump. That single trick could be broken down into many individual tricks:

1. The dog <u>sits</u> next to his owner.
2. The dog <u>stays</u> patiently while the owner tosses the dumbbell over the jump.
3. The dog <u>goes out</u> from the owner.
4. The dog <u>jumps</u> the jump.
5. The dog <u>picks up</u> the dumbbell by the middle bar.
6. The dog <u>carries</u> the dumbbell in his mouth without chewing it.
7. The dog <u>turns</u> and reorients to the owner.
8. the dog <u>comes toward</u> the owner.
9. The dog <u>jumps</u> the jump again.
10. The dog comes to a position in <u>front</u> of the owner and sits.
11. The dog <u>holds</u> the dumbbell in a seated position in front of the owner.
12. The dog <u>releases</u> the dumbbell into the owner's hand when cued.
13. The dog moves into a heel <u>position</u> when cued by the owner.
14. The dog <u>sits</u> next to the owner.
15. The dog <u>stays</u> seated next to the owner until released.

Flying Charlie!

To do a more complicated trick, your dog will need to know all of the individual parts of the trick first. Imagine if I were to try to have Charlie retrieve his dumbbell if he didn't come when called or if he was in the habit of grabbing toys and running off with them!

You and your dog have already mastered a number of behaviors that can be expanded into more complex tricks. If you've been practicing the *Bad Dog Retrieve,* you can start expanding the size, shape and texture of items that your dog will carry in his mouth. If you've been practicing the *Go to Your Mat* game, you can start sending your dog greater distances from you to his mat. If you've been doing *Hand Targeting* you can start leading your dog over jumps. (A word of caution: puppies should only do very low jumps until they're done growing.) For each new trick you choose to work on, you'll need to brush up on its component parts before stringing them together.

When you're stringing a bunch of behaviors into a chain, it's most effective to practice the last part of the trick first and then chain the rest of the behaviors on, working backwards toward the first behavior in the chain.

Kyra Sundance has a whole series of books and DVDs on teaching dog tricks. Check out her site at: www.DoMoreWithYourDog.com

You may want to make a training plan so you can better break down the components of a more advanced trick. Your dog will need to work to gain fluency in all the different aspects of the trick. Here's a sample plan for teaching a retrieve over a jump:

Dog: _____Princess_____ What does the final trick look like? Princess sits next to me while I throw the dumbbell. I send her to pick it up. She jumps the jump picks it up and brings it to me.

Trick Component Behaviors	Knows it?	Comments
Sit next to me	√	
Can stay while I throw the dumbbell		Usually
Come to front position	√	
Works off Leash		Only in fenced yard with no distractions
Carries dumbbell	√	Sometimes drops it
Send out to jump	√	She loves this!
Releases the dumbbell into my hand		Sometimes drops it a few feet away
Can get into the heel from front		

Dog:_____ What does the final trick look like?_____

_____

Trick Component Behaviors	Knows it?	Comments

Advanced Targeting

You've taught your dog to target your open hand. That trick can help you position your dog for heeling, help him to come away from distractions, and help you lead him if you're preparing to do agility with him. You can also teach him many other ways to target. If he's become used to learning with clicker training, you can teach him many behaviors very easily.

You can make a simple target stick with an inexpensive dowel and a bit of colored tape at the end to set it off visually for your dog. Present the stick near your dog's head and "click" when he gives it a sniff. Only "click " and reward when he touches the colored end of the stick. In a few minutes of consistent clicking, you should be able to lead your buddy into spins or other tricks of your choosing.

Dick and Darse are learning a new trick together.

You can teach your dog to target in many ways. He can target with his front feet, back feet, or even other parts of his body.

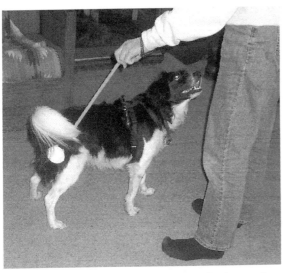

Clicker training is **very efficient**. Charlie learned to target his hip on the touch stick in less than five minutes.

It took a bit longer for Charlie to catch on to back foot targeting. It's now one of his favorite tricks.

Charlie's skateboarding skill started with foot targeting.

Charlie is very sleepy after doing a day of training demos at a big Detroit dog show.

36
"DO THE COOKIES EVER STOP?"

You'd be amazed at how many people ask this question as a criticism of positive training. "Will I always have to have cookies to have my dog behave?" Those same critics may not be able to handle their own dogs without their prong, choke or shock collars on.

The basic tenet of positive training is that the more you reward a behavior the more the behavior increases. Perhaps you had a psychology class once that taught you all about the various schedules of reinforcement that are needed to maintain a behavior; variable, fixed ratio, fixed interval, etc. Those of us who are training our dogs positively in the real world are continuing to learn from our pets as they give us feedback about the effectiveness of the training methods we are using with them. Each dog will have his

own style of learning and his own preference for rewards. Some dogs, like Reggie, will do just about anything just for a chance to be asked to do something more. Charlie likes to be rewarded by chasing and running interspersed with any kind of food, while for Kaddi, it's mostly about working for something delectable to eat.

> Karen Pryor has been the leading force in bringing clicker training to the general public . Her book *Shaping the Animal Mind, Clicker training and What It Teaches Us About Animals* is a must read!

Rewards can be many things more than just food. When I ask Charlie to sit before he goes outside, his reward for sitting is to be released to charge out the door and chase the squirrels. When I'm playing tug with Lacey, her reward for releasing the toy and sitting is the chance to be invited to play the wild game of tug again. Charlie loves to wrestle and chase the other dogs. When I call him to me, I can reward him by sending him back to play.

You'll soon notice that some tricks are your dog's favorites. You can reward your dog for one trick by asking him to do a favorite trick. The cue for doing the favorite trick becomes a reward for the first trick!

When you're shaping a new behavior, "clicking" and rewarding with food will be most efficient. As your dog gains proficiency at a new task, you can differentially reward him for outstanding performance. Also take into consideration the environment where your dogs are working. If I'm doing a program in front of a big group of wiggly kids, I'll make sure I have high value treats with me to help keep my dogs' attention.

Over time, your relationship with your dog will continue to grow. He'll enjoy spending time with you. His puppy tricks will become part of the language that you and he share. You will both be rewarded by each other's company!

37
EMPOWERMENT TRAINING

Why do we teach all the cute tricks and basic behaviors to our dog companions?

The tricks and behaviors we teach to our canine friends give us a common language they can share with us; tools to communicate with us and make us better able to share our lives together.

I want to tell you two Anja stories to illustrate my understanding of this concept.

Anja, my Smooth-Coated Miniature North American Swampdog, was highly trained. Primarily because of my involvement with Dog Scouts, I was continually motivated to systematically teach her new behaviors. She knew all the basics, come, sit, heel, and stay. I don't compete with my dogs so she wasn't drilled on these behaviors; we did it all for fun. She also learned lots of other things: ridiculously long "go outs", dexterous skills such as painting and playing musical instruments, finding my car keys hidden in the bushes, and holding poses for photography. All of those skills added to ways we could communicate with each other; ways she could "talk to me."

One day I was sitting down in the basement by the computer. Anja regularly would become impatient with my sedentary behavior. She would come down and do the "Lassie routine" of sitting cutely to get my attention, then bark and lead me upstairs, and outside. This particular day, she was especially adamant. My typical response was, "So Timmy's in the well again? Go show me what you want." This day, she didn't just take me out the back door, she led me way out into the woods. She proudly went to the base of a tree, put her feet up on the trunk and pointed up with her nose. Sitting about 20 feet up in the tree was a ground hog, the biggest "squirrel" she had ever chased up a tree. Her "empowerment" training had given her the ability to share this monumental experience with me, her human friend. Once she showed me her prize, she trotted back up to the house with me, content.

Another time, I was training a nice boxer friend in a subdivision near my home on a warm summer evening. Anja had come along for the ride and was waiting in the car while I worked with the family and their dog. The back hatch and windows of the van were open, as usual. As the lesson wound down, I went into the house with the family to chat. A few minutes later, there was a "Lassie" bark and a little scratch at the door. I was a bit surprised that Anja had left the car, but I let her into the house and she wandered around checking things out while we finished our conversation. We finally eased our way outside but were still chatting in the garage. Finally, dear Anja had had enough of my disregard for her needs. To our surprise, she purposefully walked over to a giant jug

of bottled water sitting on the garage floor, planted her foot on top of the jar, gave a bark, and stood there holding the pose (a trick from her Dog Scout *Phodography* badge). Golly was I ever stupid! My poor dog had been sitting in the car for two hours getting thirstier and thirstier while I jabbered away. She finally, in desperation, came and found me, and walked into the family's kitchen trying to find a drink on her own. When all else failed, she found her own source of water and let me know I'd better provide some of that for her!

To me, that's what empowerment training is all about. We are giving our dogs skills so they can communicate with our foreign culture; to not be prisoners bound into learned helplessness or catering to our every whim. They are our buddies and teachers. We have a mutually fulfilling relationship that grows through trust and communication.

For more information on Empowerment training, read James O'Heare's Book, *Empowerment Training*. Order the book at Dogwise.com

My hope is that the skills that you've shared working through this book will bring you and your dog to a relationship of mutual trust and understanding. I wish you the joy of mutual cooperation and friendship. Go play!

Epilogue - 3/28/2011

Charlie's been here over a year and a half now. He's still a funny little guy. He's learned to exist well in our world. He thinks he's supposed to live in my car and go everywhere with me. He's hundreds of times more responsive than he was when he first came here, but he's still his own person. Yes, he still escapes the yard. We're just lucky we live on the cul-de-sac of a traffic-free gravel road. Our spring project will be to upgrade our fencing. At least now he comes charging back to us when we call.

He's part of our family and we love him!

RESOURCES

There are many very good positive training books. I've listed some of my favorites below. To find a more comprehensive list of training books and DVDs, go to www.dogwise.com or www.clickertraining.com

Alexander, Melissa, *Click for Joy!,* Karen Pryor Clicker Training, Waltham, MA, 2003

Aloff, Brenda, *Aggression in Dogs, Practical Management, Prevention, and Behavior Modification*, Funcraft, Inc., Collierville TN, 2002

Bertilsson, Eva and Emelie Johnson Vegh, *Agility Right from the Start,* Karen Pryor Clicker Training, Waltham, MA, 2010

Burch, Mary and Bob Bailey, *How Dogs Learn,* Howell Book House, New York, NY, 1999

Donaldson, Jean, *The Culture Clash*, James and Kenneth Publishers, Berkeley, California,1997

Donaldson, Jean, *Mine!* Kinship Communications, San Francisco, CA, 2002

Grandin, Temple, *Animals Make us Human*, Houghton Mifflin, Boston, MA, 2009

Maran Graphics, *Teach Yourself Visually Dog Training,* Wiley Publishing, Hoboken, New Jersey, 2004.

Miller, Pat, *Positive Perspectives: Love Your Dog, Train Your Dog*, Dogwise Publishing, Wenatchee WA, 2003

McDevitt, Leslie, *Control Unleashed,* Clean Run Productions, South Hadley, MA, 2007

Pelar, Colleen, *Living with Kids and Dogs...Without Losing Your Mind,* C & R Publishing, Woodbridge, Virginia, 2005

Pryor, Karen, *Don't Shoot the Dog*, Bantam, New York, NY, 1985

Pryor, Karen, *Reaching the Animal Mind,* Schribner Publishing, New York, 2009

Sternberg, Sue, *Successful Dog Adoption*, Howell Book House, Indianapolis, Indiana, 2003

Stilwell, Victoria, *It's Me or the Dog* ,Hyperion Books, New York, NY, 2005

Tillman, Peggy, *Clicking with Your Dog*, Sunshine Books, Waltham, MA, 2001

Wilde, Nicole, *Help for Your Fearful Dog,* Phantom Publishing, Santa Clarita, CA, 2006

ABOUT THE AUTHOR

Beth Duman is a biologist and environmental educator who has been doing wolf education in Michigan since 1972 and has been the Michigan Representative for Wolf Park since 1974. She is one of the core trainers for Dog Scouts of America, is a Certified Professional Dog Trainer and an affiliate of Victoria Stilwell.
Her business, Earth Voices, LLC is committed to teaching compassion, fostering a world that works for everyone, with no one, human and nonhuman, left out.

She lives in Michigan with her husband Bob and four very smart dogs.

www.EarthVoices.net

Made in the USA
Charleston, SC
28 May 2011